NOTES FOR THE TEACHER

The Student Dyad Program, using student interaction, clozure, and individual pacing, has many advantages for labs and large classes. It provides the opportunity for a student to participate actively, to receive immediate feedback of correct or incorrect responses after he has responded, and to proceed at a student-selected pace. It also requires social interaction and it provides a built-in incentive for completion of the program.

In the program, the dyads provide both a cooperative and a competitive environment. "Cooperative" because students work together to assist each other in advancing through the steps of the various categories; "competitive" because students strive to complete steps before a completion deadline (the end of the semester during the tryout period) and frequently they strive to complete a step or a category before their classmates. The dyads are also mainly transactional and are thus somewhat more akin to real life situations than many English Second Language programs. The student learns prepositions, pronouns, verb forms, etc. through a constant repetition within the sentence structure. Without focusing attention on syntax, this important aspect of the language is reinforced throughout the Dyad Program as the students read and produce the thousands of sentences that constitute this program. Word order is mastered by the constant iteration of simple (and occasionally complex) English sentence patterns.

Also, the student, in a friendly situation, may have some of the individual frustrations of language learning removed by seeing that others have many of the same problems and difficulties that he has—one of the benefits listed by psychologists in group process.

MATERIAL DESCRIPTION

The materials of the program consist of a corpus of language learning material divided into categories—prepositions and related forms, pronouns and related forms and articles and determiners; verb forms and verb choices; coordinators, etc. Each of these categories has from ten to thirty-four steps, with each step having a minimum of six and as many as ten variant forms.

The steps consist of single sections having a series of unconnected sentences with fifteen clozure blanks in each section. Deleted items in the preposition category are preselected prepositions or related forms. For each blank, students select one from any two to six different stated prepositions, with review sections having unlimited choices. Deleted items in the pronoun category are preselected pronoun or related forms from various classes of pronouns, including subject, object, possessive, and reflexive. The review sections have unlimited choices from all classes previously covered. Deleted items in the verb forms category are choices of forms of *be, have, do,* and the modals. Deleted items in the verb choices category are preselected verb pairs, e.g. *do* and *make, lie* and *lay,* etc. The student's choice for clozure in all categories is determined by the context and syntax of the individual sentence.

PROCEDURAL DESCRIPTION

Students work in groups of two (dyads)—one in the role of tutor and one in the role of respondent. The copy with the correct clozure items listed at the side of the sentences is always for the tutor, and the one with the sentences with only their clozure blanks is always for the respondent, and both should be so used. In the student dyads, participants alternate as tutors and respondents. The program provides the answers, so it is not essential that the tutor know more about English than the respondent. When an odd number of students attends a session, the lab assistant or instructor acts as the tutor in one dyad.

In the operation of this program, students are assigned, when possible, to work with other students who are working in the same category and on steps near each other, with the assumption that a student tutor who had completed that step would have a good review, and a student tutor who had not yet reached that step would have a good preview and learning experience. However, it is not necessary that each member of a dyad even be in the same category. Each could work as a tutor on the respondent's program while acting as respondent on his own, thus alternating categories as well as steps. Again, both students would be learning English skills—either previewing new steps or reinforcing steps already mastered. The way through the program is through completion of the steps of each category of the program. The system is set up so any given student may be a tutor for some other student respondent either before or after he has completed the step the student respondent is on.

After the tutor and the respondent in a dyad receive their copies of the category, the respondent, holding the copy without the correct clozure

VERB CHOICES AND VERB FORMS

DYAD
LEARNING PROGRAM

STUDENT'S BOOK

Alice C. Pack

Brigham Young University
Hawaii Campus

NEWBURY HOUSE PUBLISHERS / ROWLEY / MASSACHUSETTS

NEWBURY HOUSE PUBLISHERS, Inc.

Language Science
Language Teaching
Language Learning

Rowley, Massachusetts 01969

Cover design by Christy Pizzo.
Illustrations by Ron Safsten.

Printed in the U.S.A.   First printing: October 1977
ISBN: 0-88377-079-2   5 4 3 2

items, reads the first sentence aloud indicating clozure by filling the blank, or blanks, with the correct word, or words, indicated by the sentence itself. The tutor, holding the copy with the correct clozure items listed, reinforces the respondent's clozure selection when the sentence is read by saying, "mmhmm" with rising intonation [m⌐Mm] if the item is correct, and "mm-mm" with falling intonation ['m⌐'mm] if the item is incorrect (a nonthreatening reinforcement). If the clozure item is incorrect, the respondent again reads the sentence with another selected clozure item. Students alternate as respondent and tutor in each dyad after a respondent has read all of the sentences with their clozure items in one section. Each dyad continues with alternate pages of the same step until one student makes an error-free set of responses on one of the variant forms. (The criterion for determining an error-free set of responses is the completion of a section of fifteen items without any errors on a single complete reading.) Then the student completing the step advances up one step in the program. Upon the completion of one category—that is, finishing each step in that category with an error-free page on a single complete reading—a student proceeds with another category. Students work through each category of the program step by step, from the first to the concluding step. A student may pass as many steps as he is capable of passing in any one session, or he may remain on one step for several sessions. He stays on a step until he completes a fifteen item section without an error for that step.

There may be additional choices for some of the clozures but the preference in the author's dialect is given.

VERB CHOICES

Verb choice clozure is confined to the choice between verbs which students often confuse when confronted with the selection of the correct lexical item. Many students have problems deciding whether to use *do* or *make*. They also confuse the verbs *take* and *bring*. Nearly all English second language students, and many native speakers, have trouble with *rise* and *raise*, *sit* and *set*, and *lie* and *lay*. *Bite* and *sting* have been included because Japanese students, especially, have problems as both of these are often equated with their word for *puncture*.

STEPS

1. *Do* and *make*
2. *Go* and *come*
3. *Lie* and *lay*
4. *Sit* and *set*
5. *Rise* and *raise*
6. *Bite* and *sting*
7. *Know* and *understand*
8. *Come, go* and *leave*

9. *Take* and *bring*
10. *Get, make* and *do*
11. *Say* and *tell*
12. *Want* and *need*
13. *Want* and *like*
14. *Want, need* and *like*
15. *Look, watch* and *see*
16. *Listen* and *hear*

1 A

She ——— the dress herself. At first I ———n't believe she could ——— it.

If he'd ——— his homework when it was first assigned, he'd probably ——— better grades.

He always ——— things well, and so ——— his parents.

She ——— good grades in school, and ——— a lot to help others too.

1

He ——— unhappy until he made some friends.   was

She ——— a great many opportunities in her life.   has had

He insisted that he ——— heard by the judge.   be

I would prefer that he ——— all the time he wants.   have

When we ——— young, we ——— happy.   were; were

22 G

I ——— not sure whether he will ——— there or not, as he   am; be;
hasn't ——— there lately.   been

If I ———n't sure I ——— right, I wouldn't make such a big   were; was
fuss.

Their home ——— quite small, but they ——— building a   is; are
new one.

Where ——— all the people last night?   were

He ——— with that company for a long time and will   has been
probably remain with them until he retires.

There ——— a special meeting next Monday to decide who   is;
will ——— the next chairman.   be

When ——— he here last?   was

They ——— a hard time this past year.   have had (had)

One of the boys ——— sure to win, and one of the girls ———   is; has
already won one race.

If you ——— your work promptly, I'll ——— a cake for dinner.

He ——— many things well, and so ——— his parents.

The children ——— a lot of noise during the meeting.

He was happy he ——— the team.

He ——— the best he could.

1 B

He ——— well in the tryouts and ——— the first team.

What ——— you so unhappy here?

She ——— a cake for the boy's birthday.

He ——— a bird nest of folded papers.

He always ——— that to get attention.

It ——— no difference to me which class he takes.

He usually ——— what is right.

He ——— some little animals out of the scrap lumber.

He ——— a good choice.

Usually the teachers ——— their best to help the students.

If we ——— what's right, we won't have to ———
apologies for our actions.

He frequently ——— many things that ——— his mother happy.

1 C

I ——— my bed every morning while I was there.

She ——— her homework before it's due.

22 E

I would ——— glad to help if I ——— able to.	be; were
There ——— many changes around here since you left.	have been
If I ——— the king I ——— give everyone a holiday.	were; would
The eggs ——— boiled for three minutes.	were
He is unable to come, but he ——— send a substitute.	will (can)
When ——— you take your last vacation?	did
When ——— this store open in the morning?	does
Mother says I ——— go if I finish my work.	can
One of them ——— here since 1971.	has been
It seems like we ——— here for years.	have been
This paper ——— spots on it.	has
She ——— trying to reach you for hours.	has been
They ——— a party when we arrived last night.	were having

22 F

When he ——— a little boy, he was quite handsome.	was
I would ——— glad to help if I ——— able to.	be; were
When I ——— able to, I always went to the assembly.	was
They ——— living there for several years.	have been
Sometimes he ——— some strange ideas.	has
Since you ——— there, why didn't you stop them?	were
If there ——— more people like him, the world would ——— a better place.	were; be

He ——— more money than I ——— now.

He ——— a paper bird by folding a sheet of paper.

She ——— very well in school; in fact she ——— all
A's last semester.

I cook the meals and she ——— the dishes.

She said she could ——— the dress for you next week.

He said he would ——— a canoe for you if you would
find a good log.

He ——— what is expected of him.

What ——— he ——— for a living before he came here?

How much ——— he ——— last year?

She ——— all her own clothes.

1 D

He ——— many things with his money.

She ——— a sweater with the yarn.

He always ——— his homework every night and so ——— his
friends.

They ——— him president of the group.

He ——— the work all by himself.

He ——— the toy all by himself.

She ——— her own clothes.

He ——— some kites for the boys.

She ——— that all the time.

He said he could ——— the work himself.

He ——— several mistakes on the exam.

If I were asked to run it, I would insist that the crane ——— a safety device put on it.   have

They ——— their books now and can start the lesson.   have

——— he know what is expected of him?   Does

She ———n't had that very long.   has

John ——— several accidents this past year.   has had

They ——— surprised to hear the news.   were

One of the teachers ——— absent for three days.   was

My mother and father ——— there first.   were

The clerk asked if he ——— help me.   might (could)

22 D

He could ——— a good student.   be

If he ——— happy, he'd smile.   were

He ——— problems before he came.   had (had had)

One of the boxes ——— opened when it came.   was

We ——— always had a car.   have

Mary ——— never had time to do it.   has

Why ——— they do things like that?   do

It ——— written by her father last year.   was

He ——— come whenever he ——— get off work.   will (can); can

——— you finished your work yet?   Have

I'm not sure I ——— go without permission.   should

She ——— able to do the work until she got sick.   was

See if the mail ——— delivered yet; it should ——— delivered before now.   has been; have been

Their father ——— sure the boys understood him.

If you ——— your work well you will be paid well.

He has ——— all the work required for the course.

1 E

He ——— beautiful carved figures.

She ——— beautiful dances on the program.

She asked me to ——— her a dress.

Two and two ——— four.

They usually ——— their work well.

He often ——— that.

He needs to ——— the work again.

What ——— him do that?

We have finished our work; what should we ——— now?

He said he would ——— a copy for us.

He ——— a map for the tourists.

How many mistakes did you ———?

Every day she always ——— the dishes and then ——— her bed.

He only ——— what he is told.

1 F

He ——— friends easily.

I knew she would ——— a lovely dress because she
——— everything well.

22 B

Half of these apples ——— worms in them.	have
If I had been happy I ——— have stayed.	would
It ——— a blemish so they should sell it at half price.	has
The pictures will ——— taken tomorrow morning.	be
Half of the rice ——— weevils in it.	has (had)
He ——— possibly decide to go if we buy him a ticket.	may (might)
The theme ——— changed by the committee at the last meeting.	was
What ——— the instructions say about fixing it?	do
He ——— a man now and should ——— capable of making that decision.	is; be
She ——— many problems in her home.	has
I ———n't seen him lately; I don't think he ——— around for a while.	have; has been
He ——— have tried harder.	should (could)
The bananas ——— stolen by someone in the neighborhood.	were (have been)

22 C

He ——— have been here an hour earlier to go with the first group.	should
If you want the job you ——— have to be on time.	will
What ——— the rule book say about that?	does
I have often wondered what I ——— have done in that situation.	would (could)
We ——— lots of time to finish our work before noon.	had (have)

They always ——— their homework.

He ——— his work well.

She ——— many friends while she was there.

When I see her ——— so many things well it ———
me feel small.

How many friends have you ——— here?

They have ——— several small models.

She ——— the models out of clay.

Why do you ——— that all the time?

She always ——— well in school.

Why do you ——— so many mistakes?

1 G

Her remark ——— me very happy.

His comments were ——— without too much thought.

He ——— me feel bad when he said that.

She ——— almost everything very well.

He's ——— that several times.

He's ——— several of those boats before.

I wish you'd ——— up your mind.

Would you please ——— this for me?

He ——— that all the time.

He ——— his homework yesterday.

If you think you can ——— it, why don't you try?

He ——— those all the time.

If I ——— allowed to speak I'd demand that he ——— freed.   were; be

If he ——— here he'd change things.   were

22 A   **review of all forms given**

Why ——— he always complain about things?   does

If he ——— powerful enough he would change the law.   were

Where ——— you while he ——— examined?   were; was being (was)

He knew he ——— have to do the work or he would be replaced.   would

What ——— the last conference accomplish?   did

I wish he ——— go to the conference.   could

I wish I ——— go with you, but it's impossible.   could

Some of them always ——— lots of problems.   have

The rocks ——— shaded all day long.   are

All the food had ——— eaten before we arrived.   been

He said he ——— go if he ——— possibly arrange it.   would; could

——— he always dependable?   Is

He ——— have been there because he knows everything that happened.   must

Let's —— something different for our projects.

I want to —— something of my life.

I want to —— something during my lifetime.

1 H

He has —— many mistakes in the past and will
probably —— some more.

One should —— a plan and then see if he can make
his plan work.

What —— him do that?

The boys —— a large kite.

He —— me mad when he does that.

He is —— his best.

Have you —— your work yet?

If he has —— all he can then we will —— the rest.

When he wasn't able to —— it, he quit.

How much of the work has been —— on the project?

He —— very well in the game.

He is working on his project, but he isn't —— very well.

The boys certainly —— a mess of the house.

1 I

She —— her work every day.

What have you —— to help your neighbor and
what are you planning to —— in the future?

If he ——— convicted he'd lose his job.   were

I demand that he ——— a fair trial.   have

If I ——— in your place, I'd do it.   were

He requested that he ——— transferred.   be

He wondered if he ——— dreaming.   were

She insisted that the machinery ——— a safety device.   have

I asked that he ——— given some help.   be

I felt so homesick that I wished I ——— back home.   were

He moved that the vote ——— postponed.   be

He desired that I ——— released and I know if he ——— here,   be; were
I'd be free.

If everyone ——— present we'd vote.   were

21 F

If he ——— lucky enough to win, he could quit work.   were

I demand that smoking in this room ——— stopped.   be

He requested that everyone present ——— allowed to vote.   be

She'd want to go home too if she ——— homesick.   were

They all wish they ——— back home.   were

I wish I ——— out of this situation.   were (was)

He insisted that his wife ——— allowed to talk to him.   be

She asked that she ——— given something to eat.   be

I wondered if he ——— being considered for the job.   were

I insist that he ——— the same privileges that I have.   have

I'd tell him what to do if I ——— consulted.   were

His only wish was that she ——— there too.   were (was)

You will have to ——— up your mind quickly.

If he ——— an error he will have to do his work again.

Mother ——— a pie for dinner.

Did you ——— your work?

He ———better last year in school than he is ——— this year.

She ———her little girl a dress yesterday and plans to ——— her another one tomorrow.

He told me that he was ——— his best to finish his project.

She ——— me promise that I wouldn't do that again.

Who is there among us who ——— everything right?

What did you ——— with my things?

1 J

He ——— his work well.

He ——— all the furniture in this room.

She ——— costume jewelry.

They ——— their homework last night.

We ——— a lot of things today.

She usually ——— that job.

Mary ——— all her own clothes.

Bill always ——— the dishes.

He ——— a living selling insurance.

She ——— a lot of mistakes on the exam.

Please ——— certain you haven't forgotten anything.

Bill always ——— his best.

He insisted that he ——— released.   be

The man demanded that he ——— some representation.   have

21 D

What would you do if he ——— given your position?   were

I wish I ——— ten years younger.   were

He requested that he ——— advanced in rank.   be

What would you do if it ——— your son?   were

He wished that he ——— given the same chance.   be

Her husband insisted that she ——— some time off.   have

She wishes she ——— in Europe too.   were

She requested that she ——— transferred.   be

He isn't here today, but he wishes he ———.   were

He demanded that he ——— given the right to go.   be

I'm not a doctor, but if I ——— I'd put you in the hospital.   were

If he ——— in charge he'd insist that things ——— run   were; be
differently.

I insist that they all ——— released immediately.   be

He asked that he ——— given time to consider the proposal.   be

21 E

Her mother isn't here, but if she ——— she'd fix things up.   were

If I ——— in charge, things would be different—I'd insist that   were;
the people ——— heard.   be

Mary always ——— the best she can.

How many items does that ———?

Please ——— me a favor.

1 K

I have ——— up my mind to do it.

He ——— a model of the ship.

He ——— well in his schoolwork.

She ——— a lot of good for mankind.

I think they should ——— away with all the red tape.

Your suggestion ——— sense.

Mary ——— the cooking.

He'll ——— some excuse for being late.

The president ——— the speech.

I wish she'd ——— up her mind about it.

She ———things I couldn't do.

Please ——— certain he's there.

We ——— many things while we were there.

Have you ——— your homework yet?

He ——— without a lot of things.

What would you do if he ——— in charge?   were

He requested that he ——— given a vacation.   be

He suggested that they ——— released immediately.   be

If I ——— you, I'd take his advice.   were

Supposing she ——— in my shoes; what would she do?   were

Perhaps if he ——— here, he'd do it.   were

His mother implored that her son ——— released.   be

Most of the people preferred that the man ——— a hearing.   have

21 C

I insist that I ——— allowed to call my lawyer.   be

If he ——— powerful enough he would change the law.   were

I would be glad to help if I ——— able.   were

I ask that I ——— given more time to finish.   be

If there ——— time enough we'd hear from everyone.   were

He recommended it ——— discussed at the next meeting.   be

If I ——— young again I wouldn't be as carefree.   were

If there ——— more people like him the world would be a   were
better place.

He moved that the meeting ——— adjourned.   be

If the house ——— on a hill it would have a lovely view.   were

If he ——— right we'd all be wrong.   were

I ask that he ——— given some consideration because of   be
his age.

I request that I ——— permitted to speak.   be

2 A   go, come

She ——— here frequently.

They ——— to town yesterday.

We are ——— to town tomorrow.

He is ——— to see us tomorrow before he ———.

He said he was ——— to do it, but he hasn't done it yet.

He was here a short while ago, but he's ——— now.

Be sure and ——— to the show here tomorrow night.

I don't know where they have ———.

He ——— and goes at will.

Although he was late, he ——— over anyway.

How many people plan to ——— to our party?

Everyone is ——— to our school to see the play.

He asked me when I was ——— to the show with him.

She has ——— with him several times already.

2 B

Everyone in the family ——— to school now.

They usually ——— to all their meetings.

She has ——— to see them every Sunday since she came.

How soon do you think you can ——— over?

How many times have you ——— there?

How often do you ——— swimming?

21 A   subjunctive forms

I wish I ––– able to go, but it's impossible.	were
If I ––– a millionaire, I'd buy a yacht and sail around the world.	were
If I ––– asked to comment I would insist that everyone ––– the same opportunity to speak.	were; have
If your father ––– here you wouldn't act like that.	were
The people insisted that the judge ––– impeached.	be
I sometimes wish I ––– able to live the past year over again.	were
She requested that she ––– given a hearing.	be
He demanded that the case ––– reviewed.	be
If I ––– the judge, I think I'd find him guilty.	were
If she ––– going, I'd go too.	were
He demanded he ––– given the right to speak.	be
The woman demanded that she ––– equal opportunities.	have
If he ––– happy, he'd smile.	were

21 B

I know I could do it if I ––– allowed to.	were
I'd do it if I ––– you.	were
He insisted that he ––– released.	be
The judge insisted that the man ––– an attorney.	have
If he ––– here I'd go.	were
He demanded that he ––– heard.	be
If I –––n't sure that I was right I wouldn't make such a fuss.	were

He has ——— there several times during the past month.

She never ——— unless someone takes her.

How can we ——— if the car won't run?

They ——— immediately when she called.

They are ——— out in a few minutes.

I was ——— there, but I've changed my mind.

Several people ——— to the party last night.

The medical team ——— to many countries of the world on their last trip.

The mayor ——— out of his way to help the people of his city.

2 C

I'll ——— and take my sister with me.

He ——— to see us several times.

He ——— away last year, but he's ——— back.

He never seems to seek honors; they just ——— to him.

He always ——— to see me on Fridays.

She often ——— to see her other friends too.

He ——— to school every day during the semester.

First set a goal and then ——— after it.

He never ——— to class yesterday and didn't ——— today either.

Let's ——— to the show tonight.

Who is ——— to bring the food?

All things finally ——— to an end.

He ——— to Japan for his vacation.

He would come if he could, ——— he?   wouldn't

Mary couldn't come, ——— she?   could

They brought the food, ——— they?   didn't

We'd better hurry, ——— we?   hadn't

20 F

They haven't been here very long, ——— they?   have

She doesn't sew very well, ——— she?   does

He's here every day, ——— he?   isn't

They weren't at the party, ——— they?   were

He brought the food, ——— he?   didn't

He paints very well, ——— he?   doesn't

Mary always does her homework, ——— she?   doesn't

We won't have to go, ——— we?   will

We shouldn't have to do that, ——— we?   should

You can't do that, ——— you?   can

Her parents were here, ——— they?   weren't

He has to go, ——— he?   doesn't (hasn't)

He hasn't had that very long, ——— he?   has

Bring your girl friend with you, ——— you?   won't

He wouldn't make it, ——— he?   would

327

2 D

He ——— to this place every year.

Where did he ——— yesterday?

He likes to go fishing when the tide ——— in.

She ——— to see us frequently.

Be sure and take all my things with you when you ———.

She likes to hunt for shells when the tide ——— out.

Here in the library, one must ——— in the front door and ——— out the back.

They ——— after the show started, stayed a few minutes, and ——— out before it was over.

He ——— to high school before he came here.

She ——— over to see her friend before she ——— over to see me last night.

She'll be very unhappy when he ——— back to school.

2 E

I ——— to see her yesterday for the first time.

She ——— there frequently, but I have never been.

She often ——— over here to see me.

I'd better ——— and do what he wants.

He's not sure when he's ——— abroad.

They usually ——— here for their vacation, but occasionally they ——— to the beach.

Let me know when he ——— in so I can see him.

They shouldn't furnish all the food, ––– they?	should
It doesn't flood here in the rainy season, ––– it?	does
John and Mary brought their friends, ––– they?	didn't
The washer isn't broken, ––– it?	is
They should be here, ––– they?	shouldn't
He had to go to town, ––– he?	didn't (hadn't)
They've been here before, ––– they?	haven't
He's broken his leg, ––– he?	hasn't
Mary makes her own clothes, ––– she?	doesn't
John hasn't a care in the world, ––– he?	has

20 E

They won't come, ––– they?	will
He's thought of it, ––– he?	hasn't
You'll bring it, ––– you?	won't
He's coming, ––– he?	isn't
She's swimming in the meet, ––– she?	isn't
They want to succeed, ––– they?	don't
Mary quit, ––– she?	didn't
John went to the party, ––– he?	didn't
He should go, ––– he?	shouldn't
They shouldn't be playing there, ––– they?	should
John can swim, ––– he?	can't

She ——— out for lunch at noon.

Most of the students ——— to school for ten months of the
year.

He wishes he were ——— here to school instead of ———
abroad.

Let me know when the mailman ——— as I have a letter to
post.

If he ——— before noon, bring him directly to my office;
after that I'll be ———.

2 F

When the sun ——— down, the full moon ——— up.

I'll ——— and bring my brother with me.

The train is late; it should have ——— long before now.

He often ——— to my house to see my mother.

I ——— once last year, but I'm certainly not ——— again.

I don't know why the students can't ——— to class on time
as they don't have any trouble getting ready when they're ———
on a date.

Bring all my things with you when you ———.

He brought most of my things when he ——— and took all of
his with him when he ——— back.

I don't think I will be ——— with you tomorrow.

He ——— in for a few minutes but ——— right out again.

20 C

They tried their best, ——— they?	didn't
He's not sure he can come, ——— he?	is
Many of them were late, ——— they?	weren't
He usually succeeds, ——— he?	doesn't
We're supposed to go, ——— we?	aren't
You'll be there, ——— you?	won't
We have always gone, ——— we?	haven't
He never succeeds, ——— he?	does
She's sick, ——— she?	isn't
He hasn't any, ——— he?	has
They bought it, ——— they?	didn't
He'll go, ——— he?	won't
We have some, ——— we?	don't (haven't)
The typewriters are broken, ——— they?	aren't
She has several of them, ——— she?	hasn't (doesn't)

20 D

John's father came, ——— he?	didn't
His mother isn't coming, ——— she?	is
They have a new car, ——— they?	haven't (don't)
They brought their children with them, ——— they?	didn't
He can't do that work, ——— he?	can

3 A   **lie, lay**

She is ——— on the bed.

She ——— there all day yesterday.

Just ——— the books on the table.

The books are ——— on the table.

He is ——— the silverware on the table now.

She said she would ——— the materials on the table.

I think I'll ——— here all day.

I wish he would ——— his things somewhere else.

I feel like I've ——— on this bed for weeks.

She ——— the things on the table yesterday.

I ——— there for quite awhile before I felt like getting up.

She was ——— on the bed when I saw her last.

The things were ——— on the table when I saw them last.

She was ——— the papers on the table when I came in.

The chickens ——— five eggs yesterday.

3 B

The chicken was ——— on its back.

Just ——— the eggs on the table.

I'm going to ——— down for a while.

Please don't ——— that dirty thing on my clean table.

My brother was ——— bricks for the garage.

You have lots of assignments, ——— you?	don't
They haven't come, ——— they?	have
It should be done, ——— it?	shouldn't
They don't have any, ——— they?	do
It's late, ——— it?	isn't
He won't be there, ——— he?	will
He'll be there, ——— he?	won't

20 B

They have finished, ——— they?	haven't
Some of them are here, ——— they?	aren't
She isn't here, ——— she?	is
He quit, ——— he?	didn't
He has some of them, ——— he?	doesn't (hasn't)
It's all done, ——— it?	isn't
Most of them have come, ——— they?	haven't
Mary isn't coming, ——— she?	is
You have some, ——— you?	don't
Bring yours, ——— you?	won't
He hasn't come yet, ——— he?	has
It's complicated, ——— it?	isn't
Try harder, ——— you?	won't
He passed, ——— he?	didn't
There were twenty students there, ——— there?	weren't

Your book is ——— on the hall table.

I have been ——— here on the couch all day.

He ——— the paper on the porch.

The old cemetery ——— just north of the church.

If he ——— there much longer he'll go to sleep.

He always ——— his things on that shelf.

Those things have ——— there for days.

He ——— there without moving for about twenty minutes.

He has always ——— the reports on the table.

I have seen her ——— on the beach for hours.

3 C

He has ——— there for the past three hours.

I feel like I could ——— here forever.

Where did you ——— my book?

John is ——— on the sofa in the living room.

The books are ——— all over the room.

He ———.on the bed and rested before he left.

Just ——— the package on that small table.

He said he would ——— it by the door.

You look tired. Why don't you ——— down for awhile?

The hen has ——— an egg nearly every morning.

It has ——— there for a long time.

He usually ——— down every afternoon.

If they ——— hurry we'll be late.	don't
Neither Mary nor her mother ——— be here.	will
There ——— a bit of the food left.	isn't
I ——— think about it if I were you.	wouldn't
He ——— do anything but sit there day after day.	doesn't
——— be late or we'll miss the show.	Don't
He ——— do anything to help them now.	can't
I'm sure they ——— intending to go.	weren't
Not one of them ——— here yet.	is
Why ——— she tell her mother about it?	doesn't (didn't)
Hopefully, they ——— lose their money.	won't
——— bring that up again!	Don't
That ——— have anything to do with the subject we're discussing.	doesn't

20 A   question tags

He's coming tomorrow, ——— he?	isn't
They finished their work, ——— they?	didn't
You won't be here next week, ——— you?	will
They're planning a party, ——— they?	aren't
He shouldn't do that, ——— he?	should
You're finished, ——— you?	aren't
He likes it, ——— he?	doesn't

Most of the people were ––– on their beds when the explosion occurred.

He ––– there without moving for a long time.

He ––– his books on the table and went out.

3 D

He was ––– in a hammock enjoying the breeze.

He looked like he had ––– there for hours.

He ––– there for quite awhile without moving.

Just ––– your things anywhere you'd like.

He ––– all his things on the table when he came in.

Why don't you ––– down for awhile and rest?

The storm tipped the table over and it was ––– on its side.

I haven't had a chance to ––– down all day.

She is ––– in bed and intends to stay there all day.

That old board has ––– there for the past week.

He ––– his things down and went outside.

Bring your things over here and ––– them on the table.

The old dog just ––– in the sun and never moves.

She is ––– all your things on your bed.

I can't ––– on my right side any more.

He ——— able to be here last time.   wasn't

We ——— neither the time nor the money to participate.   have

No one ——— come yet.   has

19 E

I'm not sure, but I ——— think so.   don't

Why ——— he go yesterday?   didn't

John ——— think he'll go tomorrow.   doesn't

Mary ——— go today and ——— think she'll go tomorrow   didn't; doesn't
either.

One of the boys ——— have his book yet.   doesn't

Why ——— he come last night?   didn't

I ——— have a thing to wear to the party tonight.   don't

She ——— think much of it.   didn't (doesn't)

——— he have that finished yet?   Doesn't

Why ——— he hurry up?   doesn't

Mary ——— even try to answer the questions on the test.   didn't

——— he get that finished?   Didn't

When ——— he hungry?   isn't

Why ——— he come tomorrow?   can't (shouldn't)

19 F

Why ——— they brought the things yet?   haven't

Why ——— somebody do something about it?   doesn't (didn't)

3 E

See if you can't get her to ——— down for a while.

She ——— down for a while and went to sleep.

——— your books on that shelf.

She hasn't ——— down since the storm started.

He doesn't want to ——— his things down because he might forget them.

He ——— his things down and then went off without them.

He was just ——— his things down when I came in.

She said she was just ——— down for a while.

He's been ——— there for hours.

She ——— around the house all day long without doing anything.

You hung that picture so that it's ——— on its side.

He ——— the groceries on the table and then went out.

That book is still ——— just where you left it.

She ——— in a coma for several days after the accident.

Bring your things over here where you can ——— them down.

3 F

Most of the swimmers were ——— on the sand although a few were ——— on their backs floating in the water.

I don't see how you can ——— around all day and do nothing.

I don't know where you want all these things ———; shall I just ——— them here on the bed?

Some people ——— enjoy active sports.	don't
You'd better hurry as there ——— much time left.	isn't
We ——— going with the group tomorrow.	aren't
The team ——— had much practice.	hasn't
I ——— think I'll go.	don't
Mary ——— remember what she is to bring for the dinner.	doesn't
We ——— have any assignments today.	don't
I ——— getting anywhere with my work until you helped me.	wasn't
There ——— a single one left.	wasn't (isn't)
You ——— ready for the test yet.	aren't

19 D

They never ——— come to see us.	have
She ——— been here for a long time.	hasn't
He ——— say when he was coming.	didn't
——— you see him yesterday?	Didn't
I ——— do it all by myself.	can't (won't) (shouldn't) (mustn't) (didn't)
He ——— coming tomorrow.	isn't
Why ——— you plan on going tomorrow?	don't
He ——— never been late to class.	has
There ——— been any meetings held this month.	haven't
I ——— do that if I were you.	wouldn't
There ——— many people at the last meeting.	weren't
——— he ever been late to class?	Hasn't

Why don't you ――― down for a while and rest?

I think I'm all tired out because I've ――― here so long.

Who ――― all these things on the table?

He ――― there for a long time without moving.

She was worried because her daughter just ――― there without moving.

He said he would ――― all his cards on the table.

After eating such a big meal, everyone just wanted to ――― around and rest.

She ――― around all day without doing anything; I wish you could get her to do something.

The hen ――― an egg nearly every day.

He ――― on a board at night because he says it helps his back.

4 A   **sit, set**

Ask the students to ――― down.

Most of the women usually ――― quietly and wait.

In the etiquette class we learned how to ――― the table.

The president ――― at his desk every afternoon.

The baby is ――― in his high chair.

My grandfather always ――― at the head of the table.

Every day mother ――― the china in its proper place.

John is able to ――― the spokes of the wheel just right.

Each night the astronomer ――― the telescope on Venus.

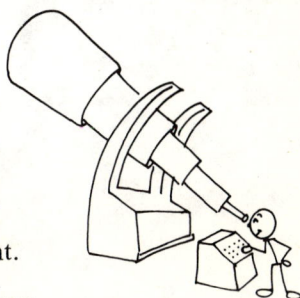

19 B

He ——— here right now.	isn't
The boy ——— work yesterday.	didn't
He ——— working now.	isn't
He ——— worked for a long time.	hasn't
There ——— anything left when I got there.	wasn't
Most of the students ——— do their homework.	didn't
——— he save any money while he was there?	Didn't
One of the boys ——— here yet.	isn't
She ——— lived here since January.	hasn't
I ——— think you're right, but I'll check.	don't
We ——— have to go unless we want to.	don't
There ——— much use for us to go now.	isn't
Neither Bill nor John ——— his work regularly.	does
There ——— many students at the assembly.	weren't (aren't)
There ——— seem to be any reason why we shouldn't go.	doesn't

19 C

He ——— being considered for the job.	isn't
We ——— heard from him for a long time.	haven't
Most of the men ——— hear the order when it was given.	didn't
One of the girls ——— come very often.	doesn't
Neither you nor he ——— nominated.	was

Everyone ——— around crosslegged on the floor at the party.

Does the director want us to ——— the stage like that?

The old hunter often ——— the meat in the freezer.

Government economists sometimes ——— prices.

He was ——— in his usual place at the head of the table.

The farmers don't usually ——— the chickens on the eggs.

4 B

When do the birds ——— in the tree?

She was ——— on the porch waiting for me.

The works of a clock can be ——— by an old watchmaker.

A sculptor's model always ——— very still.

The family must ——— still for the photograph.

The judge is old but sometimes he still ——— on the bench.

We have a TV set that just ——— and is never turned on.

I thought he ——— the prices rather high.

The letters on the printing machine are often ——— crookedly.

That old clock has ——— in that corner for years.

She ——— the hen on the eggs.

He ——— there for hours without moving.

Call the babysitter and tell her to ——— with the kids.

Barbara is so popular that she never ——— alone at lunch.

——— the food in the trays and clean the kitchen.

Some of the students ——— get their work in on time.   do

Why ——— she stay home by herself when she could be   did (does)
here with us?

——— it have to be done today?   Does

19 A   negatives—forms—
                              don't, doesn't, didn't, hasn't,
                          haven't, hadn't, isn't, aren't, wasn't,
                            weren't, won't, wouldn't can't,
                                 couldn't, shouldn't,
                              with present or past forms
                              when negative is given by
                                 never, neither, etc.

He ——— been there for a year and ——— want to go there   hasn't; doesn't
again.

My friend never ——— returned things on time.   has

I wonder why she ——— answer my letters.   doesn't

I ——— neither the time nor the money to take part in that   have
sport.

Why ——— he here yet?   isn't

I ——— go swimming because I ——— bring my bathing suit.   can't; didn't

He ——— bring the materials we need.   didn't

We ——— had much rain lately.   haven't

He ——— seem to care what happens to him.   doesn't

One of them ——— finished yet.   hasn't (isn't)

They ——— bought their texts because the book store ———   haven't; doesn't
have them in yet.

4 C

Tell the children to ——— in their places.

He ——— the furniture on the porch and it's ——— there
ever since he left.

Haven't you ——— the plates out yet?

That old man ——— in the park every day.

That girl ——— at home every night.

——— the pencils in the drawer.

That old couch has ——— there for years.

They often ——— there hour after hour.

The mechanic was able to ——— the gears of the car in place.

The guard ——— in the guard shed every night.

Who ——— the prices on this food?

Why don't you ——— the chair on the floor?

Every day the bird watcher ——— the binoculars on his favorite
tree.

No one ——— there any more.

4 D

Why don't you ——— over there in the easy chair?

Grandpa ——— in that chair every day while he was visiting.

The baby can't ——— alone yet.

He was ——— on that limb of the tree when he fell.

——— your things down for a while and rest.

Why ——— he take so much time?   did (does)

Although he can't go he ——— want to be invited.   does

——— everybody want to go?   Does

——— we have to finish this before we can go?   Do

Why ——— you come home so late last night?   did

Where ——— this river run to?   does

Where ——— all the food you bought go?   did

Mary won't call, nor ——— she want anyone to call her.   does

Why ——— you do it all by yourself?   did

I don't care what she says, I know I ——— call her.   did

I ——— want to be remembered by all of you.   do

18 F

——— your father have all the help he needs?   Does

I ——— want to call her today sometime.   do

Why ——— she always call me at work?   does

That boy really ——— think a lot of you.   does

Where ——— all the time go to?   did (does)

Where ——— you spend your vacation last year?   did

Why ——— they do that?   did

I ——— listen to my parents occasionally.   do

Mary ——— think a lot of him at one time.   did

What time ——— the sun rise in the morning?   does

——— your friend go with you on the hike?   Did

——— any of the students ever get there on time?   Do

He ——— that machinery up every day.

He was ——— up the materials when he fell.

She ——— down very hard when the chair broke.

She is ——— over there in the corner pouting.

Everything was all ——— up ready for us.

He has ——— there for a long time without speaking.

He usually ——— the firewood up a certain way so it will catch fire easily.

Who ——— behind you in class?

Grandpa always ——— in this chair.

I wonder who will ——— at the head of the table.

4 E

She ——— the things on the table yesterday.

Every night his wife ——— the food on the table.

——— down in that chair over there.

She is ——— for her portrait.

He's just ——— there reading the newspaper.

She ——— there for quite a while before she got up.

The printer's devil ——— the type for the newspaper.

She's ——— in the corner all by herself; I wish someone would go over and ——— by her.

He just ——— on the chair and never said a word.

She is ——— the table for dinner now.

You must ——— very still or the picture will be blurred.

18 D

I really ——— think it's a good idea. What ——— you think of it?	do; do
Perhaps he ——— want it after all.	does
When ——— the train leave?	does
When ——— John and Mary expect to go?	do
Why ——— they always take so long?	do
Why ——— the project take so long to finish?	did
Where ——— they go on their vacation?	did
——— I have to finish this today?	Do
Why ——— I have to finish it so soon?	do
I ——— think about it, but I still don't want to go.	did
He ——— listen to his parents, but he still has to make up his own mind about things.	does
What time ——— the plane usually come?	does
Why ——— they leave everything with you?	did
He ——— say he would do it.	did

18 E

Why ——— he always do it that way?	does
I ——— want to go although I'm afraid I can't.	do
——— she do everything she could to prevent the accident?	Did
He really ——— like you very much.	does

He ——— his things down and went over and ———— in the hammock.

I don't think the children can ——— still.

4 F

The food ——— there and no one touched it.

They ——— the stage for the play.

The prices are ———— by someone else.

He sometimes ——— there for hours without speaking.

She ——— the food on the table, but no one touched it.

She ——— there for quite a while without moving.

——— the clock so it shows the correct time.

He was just ——— there when I saw him last.

I have ——— here so long I'm stiff.

She was ——— the music for the concert on the stands.

All the students came in quietly and ——— down.

The old clock just ——— on the shelf; it has ——— there since grandmother brought it here.

Have you ever ———— for a portrait?

The old cat just ——— there and licks her paws.

I'm sure he ——— think about serious things occasionally.	does
Where ——— they live?	do
When ——— the performance start?	does
——— these things interest you?	Do
——— you attend the meeting yesterday?	Did
——— you think you can do it?	Do
What ——— he tell them about the project?	did
I've already told you, I ——— too do it.	did
What ——— the rule book say about that?	does
What ——— the instructions say about fixing it?	do

18 C

Why ——— he always complain about things?	does
When ——— you take your last vacation?	did
——— this place appeal to you?	Does
Why ——— people act the way they ———?	do; do
When ——— the next train leave for the city?	does
——— they get all their work done on time?	Did
——— he ever get there on time?	Does
Where ——— everyone at the picnic come from?	did
It really ——— matter to me what you say.	does
Why ——— the trains always arrive at the same time?	do
Where ——— the money for the project come from?	does (did)
I ——— think it matters.	do
What ——— the last conference accomplish?	did
I'm telling you again, I ——— complete my work yesterday.	did

5 A   rise, raise

The sun ——— in the east.

They ——— the new flag over the capitol.

Everyone ——— when the President comes in.

He ——— from his chair when she came in.

They have ——— flowers for years.

He ——— prize flowers for a hobby.

It's customary to ——— your hand before asking a question.

He ——— early every morning.

The sun ——— at 7 A.M. and set at 6 P.M. today.

Why don't you ——— the window and let in some air?

The contractor said they would be ——— the walls on the new building soon.

The flag ——— slowly as the people sang the National Anthem.

He ——— the heavy weights and won the contest.

He ——— and lowers the flag every day.

I like to watch the moon ———.

5 B

My friend always ——— when women come into the room.

It's warm in here. Please ——— the window.

The sun ——— at 7:15 yesterday morning.

He ——— his hand but the teacher didn't call on him.

Yeast makes the bread ———.

18 A   *do* as auxiliary—
                                       do, does, did

——— you think he should go tomorrow?	Do
——— he go yesterday?	Did
——— his roommate have a book he could loan him?	Does
——— we have to go to the meeting today?	Do
——— you go yesterday? I ———.	Did; did
When ——— this store open in the morning?	does
What time ——— the sun go down at night?	does
Why ——— she stay home last night instead of coming to the party?	did
I certainly ——— do my work yesterday.	did
What ——— all of the boys think about this?	do
People ——— listen to him occasionally.	do
Why ——— that always have to happen when we're in a hurry?	does
——— John have all the material he needs?	Does
——— I have to do it today?	Do

18 B

Why ——— she do things like that?	does
——— you think you could do it?	Did (Do)
——— he know what is expected of him?	Does
Why ——— they do things like that?	do
Mary doesn't sing nor ——— she play the piano.	does

I ——— early this morning and took a long walk.

He ——— the flag as the group sang the National Anthem.

The water ——— with the tide.

My father ——— many different crops.

He always ——— early.

When he gives you the signal ——— the banner.

When he came into the room everyone ——— to his feet.

My father has ——— a big wheat crop for several years.

At dinnertime the smoke ——— from all the chimneys.

She was unable to ——— from her chair.

5 C

He is ——— wheat on his acreage this year.

Why didn't you ——— your hand to answer that question?

The sun and the moon both ——— in the east.

Why didn't you ——— when she came into the room?

He ——— lots of corn last year.

The bread ——— to double its bulk in an hour.

She is ——— her family without any outside help.

They ——— the flag at 8 o'clock.

The flag ——— quickly when he pulls the ropes.

During the past hour the bread has ——— to twice its bulk.

He has ——— and lowered the flag every day since he came.

He is ——— to great heights in his company.

I ——— too much to do since I came here.	have had
He ——— called before the committee.	was
I ——— not take any more time off this week.	can (will)
He might ——— finished first if he ——— run harder.	have; had
He ——— that old car for years.	has had
I ——— like to have seen the game, but it was impossible to get away.	would
One of my parents ——— called every day.	has

17 F

I wish he ——— come back and given us a report.	had
They ——— a party next week to celebrate.	are having
Both of them ——— finished the exam already.	have
Our team ——— the best of all those who competed.	was
Why ———n't you finished your work?	have
He ——— trying to upset us.	was
She ——— aware of the consequences when she did it.	was
He ——— a successful businessman ever since he graduated.	has been
They ——— coming tomorrow at three o'clock.	are
No one in the class ——— finished the assignment.	has
She is the only one who ——— any trouble.	is having (has had)
Everyone ——— plenty of time to do the assignment.	has had
He might ——— come if he ——— encouraged to do so.	have; had been
The least she ——— have done was to call me.	could

When the boy let out the string the kite ——— high above the buildings.

They ——— the roofing material to the top floor by means of a pulley.

He always ——— early in the morning.

5 D

Hot air usually ——— to the top of the room.

The smoke ——— rapidly after he lit the fire.

He ——— his hand before he asked the question.

It's hard to ——— potatoes here.

He ——— early and went for a walk.

The bread has ——— high enough to put in the oven.

When the president came in, everyone ——— to his feet.

If you'd ——— the blinds it would be lighter in here.

He tried hard to ——— the heavy weights.

Let's go for a walk and watch the moon ———.

They ——— and lower the flag by means of a pulley.

When they voted on the question, we all ——— our hands.

They have ——— the price for the show.

I don't think any fish will ——— to that bait.

Every morning he ——— early and goes jogging.

17 D

One of the girls ——— late this morning.	was
Half of the students ——— unhappy with the present program.	are
They ——— planned to go yesterday but ——— unable to make it.	had; were
He ——— finished before I ———.	was; was
There ——— too many accidents around here.	have been
The sun ——— too hot to go outside yesterday.	was
The man who ——— speaking is my father.	is (has been)
He could ——— tried for his crimes.	be (have been)
He ——— have been punished.	should (could)
He ——— a hard time trying to convince her that he ——— do the job.	has had; can
Where ——— you yesterday?	were
——— Nancy prepared for her talk last week?	Was

17 E

We ——— a late lunch when he called.	were having
Come and see me when you ——— more time.	have
They ——— a lot of practice this past month, so they should ——— in top condition.	have had; be
One of the girls ——— some trouble with her back this past week.	has had
He ——— planning on coming tomorrow.	is
I ——— all mixed up about the plans.	am

5 E

At eight o'clock the bell rings, the flag ———, and everyone sings the National Anthem.

He was so weak he could scarcely ——— his hand.

That picture needs to be hung higher; why don't you ——— it about six inches?

Gentlemen used to ——— when ladies came into a room.

She enjoys her garden and ——— some lovely flowers.

The building is ——— rapidly.

They expect to ——— their prices.

He has ——— a number of questions about the project.

When the curtain ———, the show is about to begin.

He ——— the flag in his hand and waved it wildly.

He is ——— wheat on his farm.

They ——— the car with a block and pulley.

I don't think anyone ——— that question.

I think I'll ——— early tomorrow and go for a hike.

The balloon was ——— rapidly above the crowd.

5 F

He was always the first one to ——— his hand when a question was asked.

He will ——— to great heights in politics.

She always ——— wonderful tomatoes.

He ——— before the cock crows in the morning.

I ——— have gone if I'd wanted to.   could

He should ——— told us about it.   have

When do you think we ——— go?   can (should)

He ——— some marvelous experiences in his past life.   has had

We ——— always happy then.   were

He hasn't ——— back since he left.   been

All of the students ——— on time this morning.   were

Many years ——— passed since then.   have

17 C

He ——— there last week when we ———.   was; were

We ——— more practice than he ———.   have had; has

We ——— have gone if we had known about it.   would (could)

He ——— there more often than I have.   has been

I ——— go if you go.   will (can)

The food ——— eaten very quickly.   was

He should ——— gone to the meeting.   have

I ——— waiting for a long time and I'm tired.   have been

One of the girls ——— late for the practice last night.   was

Most of the girls ——— on time every day.   are

He ——— a lot of trouble since he came.   has had

When ——— she here last?   was

The temperature ——— rapidly after the sun came out.

She ——— the hem on her dress because it was too long.

The ducks ——— quickly from the pond and were soon out of sight.

They ——— the flag every morning over the schoolhouse.

He has ——— vegetables for years.

She has ——— early all her life.

The kite ——— so high we could scarcely see it.

Why did you ——— when he came into the room?

He is ——— a big fuss about the new rule.

Steam is always ——— from the hot pools.

They have ——— the price for the show.

6 A   bite, sting

The mosquitoes ——— me while I was at the picnic.

A bee ——— me yesterday.

Be careful or that dog will ——— you.

That's a wasps' nest, be careful you don't get ———.

This won't hurt, but it may ——— a little.

If a poisonous snake ——— you, it can be fatal.

I wouldn't like that bumblebee to ——— me.

He was ——— by a scorpion.

17 A
review of all forms
previously given

We ——— here for hours.	have been
I ———n't seem him lately; I don't think he ——— around.	have; has been
He ——— here several times before I left.	had been (was)
They ——— ready to begin right now.	are
I'm sure he ——— happier before.	was
He ——— a lot of problems.	has had
He ——— a man now and should ——— capable of making that decision.	is; be
Where ——— you while he ——— examined?	were; was being (was)
He ——— problems before he came here.	had had (had)
——— you finished your work yet?	Have
He could ——— a good student.	be (have been)
These shoes ——— a good fit.	are

17 B

I wish I ——— remember her name.	could
He ——— here for a little while, but I don't know where he ——— now.	was; is
She hasn't ——— much fun this past year.	had
Ask her if she ——— go tomorrow.	can
He ——— here ever since I can remember.	has been
This will ——— remembered for a long time.	be

When it opened its mouth, I was afraid the animal
would ——— me.

She screamed when the bee ——— her.

Cleopatra died when a snake ——— her.

He has several large welts where the mosquitoes ——— him.

How many times have you been ——— by a bee?

A mosquito ——— a man and gets nourishment from his
blood, while a bee ——— him and dies.

6 B

They have a mean dog who ——— anyone who enters the yard.

The medicine ——— when he put it on my sore.

I didn't see the mosquito which ——— me.

A bee can only ——— once.

He has a toothache and can't ——— anything.

He was very ill because a scorpion ——— him.

He says the rash on his arm ———.

It doesn't really hurt, it just ———.

He was ——— by the dog when he went into the yard.

That dog is mean; he ———.

Have you ever been ——— by a mosquito or ——— by a wasp?

Bees only ——— when they are disturbed.

The last time I was in Florida I was ——— by a bee and ———
by dozens of mosquitoes.

Mother says I ——— go if I finish my work.   may (can)

I ——— like to go, but my work isn't finished.   should (would)

I'm not sure I ——— go without permission.   should

I wish I ——— go with you, but it's impossible.   could

16 F

I ——— go if I had the opportunity.   would

Bring them over here so we ——— count them all.   can

It ——— happen although it has never happened before.   could

If she had liked the country she ——— have stayed.   would

I ——— go immediately or I ——— be too late and I really   must; might
———n't want to miss it.   (will); would

If he is elected he ——— do a good job.   would (could)
                                                                      (should)

He ——— have been here before now; we really ———n't   should; can
wait any longer.

It ——— never have happened if you had been here.   would (could)
                                                                      (might)

If you go I think I ——— probably go with you.   should (will)

If he were here he ——— know what to do.   would

——— anyone who wants to enter the contest?   Can

If he had been here he ——— have fixed things up.   might (could)

6 C

I was afraid the dog would ——— me.

What happened when the bee ——— you?

He hopes the fish will be ——— today.

She yelled when the wasp ——— her.

Use some repellent so the mosquitoes won't ——— you.

He was ——— several times by a ferocious dog.

The bees have ——— him before.

My arm ——— where the mosquito ——— me.

He was ——— by a manta ray while he was swimming.

Those fish will ——— at anything.

Does your dog ———?

Where did the bee ——— you?

A bee ——— when he is disturbed.

He's a very friendly dog; I don't think he'll ——— you.

6 D

It ——— when I put the medicine on.

The fish are ——— today.

It itches where the mosquitoes ——— me.

Have you ever been ——— by a dog?

Be careful or those bees will ——— you.

It ——— when the doctor gave me a shot.

——— I enter the contest? | May (Can) (Could) (Should)

I ——— go immediately or I ——— be late again. | must; will

If I am elected I ——— do my best to serve. | will (shall)

He ——— have been here an hour ago; I don't think I ——— wait any longer. | should; can (shall)

It ——— never have happened if I had been there. | would (could) (might)

When he goes I ——— probably go with him. | shall (will)

Wherever she is I ——— try to find her. | shall (will) (should)

If he were here he ——— do the right thing. | would

16 E

They ——— never have done it if I had been there. | would

If I had been the king I ——— have given everyone a holiday. | would

How many times ——— we forgive others? | should

If I had been happy I ——— have stayed. | would

If I were the king I ——— give everyone a holiday. | would

If I am elected I ——— do my best to serve. | shall (will)

He ——— have been here an hour ago. | should

We ——— find her at home if she isn't at the office. | may (might)

Most of the students ——— have done better on the exam. | could (should)

I ——— be there tomorrow if they need me. | can

He ——— possibly decide to go if we buy him a ticket. | may (might)

These large mosquitoes really ———.

He's a vicious dog—he ———.

While he was there a centipede ——— him.

Some people are allergic and have severe swelling when a bee ——— them.

The boy was hungry and quickly ——— into his sandwich.

Have you ever been ——— by a scorpion?

The alcohol ——— when I put it on the wound.

I wish the fish would ——— today.

If a bee ——— anyone, it dies.

6 E

She was ——— by a bee yesterday.

That dog is really mean. He has ——— me twice.

This medicine may ——— a little when I put it on.

Did the bee ——— you?

The wasps were ——— everyone at the picnic.

Don't feed the bears or they might ——— you.

She was ——— several times by yellow jackets.

When these mosquitoes ———, they leave large welts.

I wish the fish were ——— today.

Put some lotion here where the mosquito ——— me.

The bees buzzed angrily around but didn't ——— anyone.

Have you ever been ——— by a centipede or ——— by a scorpion?

16 C

He ——— have been here an hour earlier to have gone with the first group.	should
I ——— have finished my work last night because I have no time today.	should
I think I ——— have won if I had entered the race.	could (would)
I'm sure he ——— do the job if he tries.	can
He is not sure whether he ——— go or not; he ——— have to ask permission.	can; will
——— I have permission to go with them?	May (Can)
She ——— have enjoyed going with them and ——— have if she had known in time.	would; could
If you want to keep the job you ——— have to work hard.	will
She said she ——— come whenever she gets off work.	will (can)
If I had been there I ——— have helped her.	would (could)
If I had been the king I ——— have given everyone a holiday.	would
He ——— be here in an hour; we'll have to hurry with our work or we ———n't go with him.	will; can

16 D

I ——— go if I were you.	would
If I were the king I ——— give everyone a holiday tomorrow.	would
Ask your mother if you ——— go.	may (can)
It has never happened before, but if things were just right it ——— happen.	might (could)
If I had been happy I ——— have stayed.	would

That dog is always ——— people.

Did many bees ——— you while you took out the honey?

6 F

I don't like bees; they ———.

It really doesn't hurt—it just ——— a little.

If the dog hadn't been chained, it would have — —— me.

You'll really be sick if you're ——— by a manta ray.

It was a large centipede which ——— him.

Be careful as there are snakes around which might ———.

Bees ——— when they are disturbed.

If there's a mosquito around, it will ——— me.

He broke his tooth when he ——— into the hard candy.

The fish aren't ——— today.

When a mosquito ———, it sometimes ———.

The manta ray ——— him when he stepped on it.

Be careful of the scorpions; they ———.

They took him to the doctor when the centipede ——— him.

He ——— come whenever he ——— get off work.	will; can (could; would)
See if you ——— arrange your affairs to be there.	can
If I had been there I ——— have helped her.	would (could)

16 B

He knew he ——— have to do the work or he would be replaced.	would
He ——— have come but he didn't want to.	could
He knew he ——— study or he'd fail the course.	must
He is unable to come, but he ——— send a substitute.	will (can)
He didn't know whether he ——— come or not.	could
I don't think I'd worry about it; however, it ——— be important to someone else.	could
It ——— have been a disaster, but everything turned out all right.	could
Everything ——— have been wonderful if you had been there.	would
I have often wondered what I ——— have done in that situation.	would
——— I go with you?	May (Can)
He ——— have been there because he knows everything that happened.	must
He ——— have tried harder.	should (could)
Things ——— have been different if he had been able to go to school.	might
He ——— be here tomorrow if he can.	will
I ——— learn what is expected of me or I'll lose my job.	must

7 A   **know, understand**

Do you ――― the way to the airport?

Although I've read the chapters, I still don't ――― the lesson.

I don't ――― either of them; they're strangers to me.

I don't ――― math at all.

He ――― how to drive a car but he isn't a very good driver.

Because he once lived in a ghetto, he ――― the feelings of those who live there now.

I ――― how to crochet, but I can't ――― the directions.

Do you ――― the rules of the game?

Do you ――― how to ride a horse?

I can ――― the directions, but I still don't ――― how to finish it.

I thought I ――― what he said even though he was speaking in another language.

I ――― it by heart, but I forgot it when I saw the huge crowd.

He ――― better than anyone else what is expected of him.

7 B

I thought I ――― the lesson, but I flunked the exam.

I couldn't ――― him because he spoke too softly.

Althouth I've ――― him for years, I really don't ――― him.

I don't ――― how to do that math problem.

If he ——— spare the money, we ——— certainly use it.	could; could (would)
They bought some new furniture although they really ———n't afford it.	could
We ——— have expected him to do that.	might
The show ——— be over by now.	should
It looks like it ——— rain.	might (could)
Do whatever you think ——— be done.	should
You ——— have thought of that before you came.	should
He ——— do anything for her.	would

16 A **modals, present and past—**
can, could, shall, should, may,
might, will, would, must

He ——— have known he would get into trouble.	might (should)
He ——— have been here an hour earlier to go with the first group.	should
I ——— have finished my work last night because I have had no time today.	should
I think I ——— have won if I had entered the race.	could (would)
I'm sure I ——— do the job; just let me try.	can
If I had been there earlier I ——— have gone with them.	could (might)
I'm not sure I ——— go; I ——— have to ask permission.	can; will
——— I have permission to go with them?	May
I ——— have enjoyed going with them.	would
If you want the job you ——— have to be on time.	will

He ——— how to drive a car, but he wasn't a
very good driver.

Because he has never lived in a ghetto, he can't
——— the feelings of those who live there.

I couldn't ——— the directions.

Do you ——— how to type?

I thought I ——— the directions, but I don't ——— how to
construct the model.

I ——— what he's saying even though he's speaking in another
language.

I ——— his situation, but I really don't ——— how to help him.

He ——— what is said to him, but he doesn't ——— how to
answer.

7 C

I ——— the formula, but I don't ——— how it works.

Did you ——— the question on the exam?

He says he can't ——— the younger generation.

I think I ——— how it works, but I don't ——— for sure.

Some students have an accent and it's hard to ——— them.

I wish I ——— what he said in his talk; unfortunately, I don't
——— Japanese.

How much do you ——— about their plans?

He ——— most of the students well, and he's ——— many of
them for years.

15 E

I thought he ――― swim better than that.	could
If he had told me about it, I ――― have been able to help him.	might
He ――― speak English well because he's studied it for years.	should
I ―――n't do that again for any amount of money.	would
Everyone ――― attend the meeting this afternoon.	should
He ――― have discussed it with me before he sent in the report.	should (could)
It ――― not sell because of the flaw in it.	might
I ――― have helped him if I ――― have.	would; could
He ――― apply for the job early if he really wants it.	should
If he ――― do his best, I know he ――― succeed.	would; could (would)
When you bring the things over, I ――― like to see them.	would
He ――― bring his class over to see the program.	might (could) (should)
Most of the students ――― like to see their grades.	would

15 F

What ――― you do if that ever came up?	would (could)
I don't know what ――― have been done that wasn't.	could
We ――― support her by going to the concert tonight.	should
Don't get wet or you ――― catch cold.	might
The plumber ――― repair the pipe before noon.	should
We ――― have brought a map; now we're lost.	should

How well did you ––– the lecture?

I ––– the facts but didn't ––– how much they meant.

7 D

I wish I ––– what he was talking about.

He mumbles so that I can rarely ––– him.

Could you ––– the teacher this morning?

He ––– the whole thing by heart.

She thought she ––– all the facts, but she didn't.

Do you ––– how that machine works?

I don't ––– how to help him although I really
––– his situation.

He thought that no one ––– him.

He ––– the rules, but he didn't obey them.

I'm sure she ––– what's right and what's wrong.

He says he doesn't ––– anyone here.

Listen carefully and try to ––– what he says.

I know he ––– me when I spoke to him.

I thought I ––– the speaker, but I'm not sure.

65

I ———n't think he'd want to go.   should

He ——— surprise you and do better than you think.   might

He promised he ———n't do it any more.   would

How many pencils ——— there be in a box?   should

You ——— count them if you wanted to.   could

I said I ——— try and be there on time.   would

If you ——— make up your mind then we ——— give them
our decision.   would; could

15 D

I ——— like to have gone, but I didn't have the money.   would

I don't think it will, but it ——— happen.   might (could)

He never ——— remember figures, even when he was young.   could

You ——— have answered her letter before you left.   should

What ——— have happened if you hadn't helped him?   would

You ——— do your homework every night.   should

If I thought I ——— help you, I ———. You know that.   could; would

I ——— have known you'd be right.   might (should)

You ——— have known better.   should

What ——— a person do when something like that comes up?   should

I ———n't do anything to help myself as I was helpless.   could

What ——— you have done in my situation?   would

They ——— have been here by now.   should

I wonder who ——— have helped them with the problem.   could

7 E

It isn't necessary to ——— how it works if you ——— how to run it.

I ——— he was listening, but I don't think he ——— what was said.

He said he ——— everyone at the party.

He ——— more than anyone thinks he does.

I thought you ——— how to fix this.

I think I'll drop the class as I don't ——— anything.

Can't you ——— me when I talk?

I ——— he'll do whatever you tell him to.

She said she would read the instructions and try to ——— them.

I still can't ——— why she did that.

I don't ——— what he'll do next.

Many of them seem confused and don't ——— what to do.

He ——— enough not to do that.

7 F

I can't ——— anything about him.

She ——— I want to see her, but she avoids me.

Most of them ——— what they wanted.

I have ——— him for years.

She said that no one ——— her.

15 B

Both of us ——— have known better than to do that.	should
I ——— have gone if I'd wanted to.	could
Because of my busy schedule I really ———n't take the time to go. However, I'm going.	should
He ——— have finished that piece long ago if he'd tried.	could
I ——— consider going if all my expenses were paid.	might
When ——— we plan on leaving to get there on time?	should
I ———n't get away any sooner although I had planned to leave earlier.	could
Although he tried he ———n't make it.	could
I ——— like to go to the dance tomorrow.	should (would)
When do you think you ——— do it for me?	could
He doesn't seem to be able to do it although I thought he ———.	could
We ——— try and observe all the rules while we're here.	should
I said I ———, although I wasn't sure.	could
He ——— have told me about it earlier so I ——— have done something about it.	should (might); could

15 C

They ——— have left earlier, but the car wasn't ready.	could (might)
Many of the boys ———n't make it today.	could
I ——— have been there, but I ———n't arrange the time.	should; could
If I ——— have helped him I ——— have.	could; would
I'm not so sure, the other team ——— beat us.	might (could)

Can you ——— what she's trying to say?

I ——— what he wants even if I can't ——— him.

I thought I ——— the directions, but I don't ——— what to do now.

I'm sure he ——— everything we're saying.

I ——— he wants to come, but he won't ——— anything at the convention.

Can you ——— these directions?

He should have ——— what was expected of him.

8 A   come, go, leave

My father usually ——— for work at 7:00 a.m., but this morning he didn't ——— until 9 o'clock.

It's a beautiful spot; we must ——— here when it isn't raining.

I need to ——— to the store today.

He ——— to work early this morning.

He often ——— into our room to show us his new books before he read them.

We must ——— here before it starts raining.

Mary has to ——— home early in the morning to get to school on time.

Our neighbors ——— over to visit us once a week.

John ——— to the movies almost every week while he was in school.

My mother says I ——— go if your mother ——— let you go.   may (can); will

He ——— have been blind not to see that car coming.   must

I ——— report this to my supervisor.   shall (must) (will)

He's not sure whether anyone ——— get away this afternoon.   can (will)

15 A   modals, past—
could, should, might, would

He asked if he ——— help us.   could (might)

I wasn't sure whether I ——— offer to help or not.   should

I ——— go if I ——— arrange things at home.   would (could); could

There's a possibility that he ——— have been working here last year.   might (could)

If I thought I ——— have done it, I ——— have tried.   could; would

I ——— always study better when I lived at home.   could

I ——— rather have hired Bill but he wasn't available.   would

You ——— have asked for a recommendation.   should (could) (might)

They ———n't give the workers a raise so a strike was called.   would

He ——— rush to the door when his father came home.   would

He ———n't find work there last summer.   could

He ———n't finish the work because he was ill.   could

I think we ——— leave right away.   should

277

Sometimes I ——— to class without my books.

The mailman ——— at about 11:00 a.m. every day.

The bus to Honolulu ——— in this direction.

You must ——— there some day when it isn't raining.

His father ——— home from work very late every
night last week.

8 B

John ——— for class at 7:15 a.m, so he should be on time.

He always ——— with a new girl.

Mary feels sick so she's ——— early.

This morning she ——— the house early to see the doctor.

She was late as she ——— to class at 9:00 o'clock this morning.

Our friends never ——— over to visit us.

The doctor ——— home from his office and then ——— out
again immediately.

My sister ——— to the mainland last year for a short visit, but
——— back again to go to school.

Mary ——— here two months ago and ——— to New York.

You've missed your friend; he ——— about five minutes ago.

We missed each other; he ——— out one door and I ——— in
the other.

14 E

If I ——— make it, I'll be there by four o'clock.	can
He says he ——— definitely finish the project.	will
I ——— or ——— not go; it depends entirely on the weather.	may; may
They say they ——— pay well if someone ——— do the job.	will; can
Some of the students ——— leave tomorrow, but others ——— complete some assignments before they ——— go.	will; must; can
If he has time he ——— go with you.	may (can) (will)
I have definitely decided I ——— accept the job.	shall (will) (can)
My sister is planning to go if she ——— get the money.	can
I ——— arrange to pay for it, but I ———n't find the time to go.	can; can
We ——— seriously consider your proposition.	shall (will)

14 F

I told him he ——— finish the assignment immediately.	must
I ——— certainly go if I have the opportunity.	shall (will)
They ——— see the ocean from their house.	can
He says he ——— leave most of his things here until he comes back.	will (can) (must)
Bring me some lunch when you come back if you ———.	can
They say we ——— take two bags with us if we ——— carry them both.	may; can
She ——— have lived here at one time.	may
They ——— travel extensively this year.	will (can)
He says he ——— swim well.	can

8 C

My father ——— for work at 7:00 a.m. although he usually doesn't leave until 9.

I have ——— to the store every day for the past week.

He ——— to work at 7:00 every morning last week.

The bus ——— Kahuku every 30 minutes.

Sometimes he ——— into our room to show us a new book.

It started to rain after we ———.

Mary ——— home early in the morning to get to school on time.

Our neighbors used to ——— over and visit us every week.

John ——— to the movies almost every week.

Sometimes I ——— my books at home, but I'm usually sorry I ——— without them.

You must ——— here some day when it isn't raining.

His father ——— home from work very late every night.

Many of the students ——— from a foreign country and were homesick.

8 D

John ——— for class at 7:15 a.m. every morning.

The professor ——— into the room and showed us a new book.

Mary felt sick yesterday afternoon, so she ——— home from the office early.

Bert ——— to his class at 8 o'clock, but it was a holiday.

The new neighbors ——— to visit them regularly.

He thinks he ――― go, but he's not sure.   can

――― I ask your name, please?   May

If you ――― provide a car, I ――― bring the food for the   can (will);
picnic.   will (can)

I ――― predict one thing about the race. Our car ―――   can (will);
beat yours.   will

Many of the students ――― drop the course before the end   will
of the semester.

14 D

I ―――n't be there before noon but ――― come as soon as   can; will
possible.

The work ――― wait until you get back.   can (will)

I ――― not come here again.   shall (will)
                                                                         (may) (must)

When ――― the visitors arrive?   will

They ――― be here soon.   will

He ――― do it by himself if he tries.   can

I ――― get this done immediately or it will be too late.   must

He is sure he ――― do it alone.   can

He ――― bring the things with him.   will (must)

I ――― do it soon, but I ―――n't give you the exact time.   will (can); can

Ask your mother if you ――― go with us.   may (can)

He says he ――― come as soon as he possibly ―――.   will; can

273

Our friends ――― over to visit us.

My sister ――― home late from work.

John ――― to school on the mainland last year.

He ――― Utah in April and ――― over here to live.

She missed the bus; it ――― five minutes ago. However, another one should ――― in about thirty minutes.

We will have a big crowd to register if everyone ――― at the same time.

I don't think I can ――― with you this week as I ――― every day last week.

8 E

He ――― out just a little while ago, but should be ――― back before long.

He ――― for work early this morning.

The bus to Honolulu ――― from that direction.

I'm afraid you've missed him; he ――― about an hour ago.

The bus is ――― to pick us up.

The bus for town is ――― in half an hour.

He has ――― out, but should be back before long.

When he ――― in be sure and tell him I need to see him.

He seems to ――― out every time I ――― in.

She ――― here and ――― to California.

Be sure and take your things with you when you ―――.

He never ――― over to see us any more.

We missed him when he ――― away.

14 B

I'll see if I ——— arrange to do it for you.	can
I ——— go if I receive an invitation.	shall (will) (can) (may) (must)
The office ——— be closed by then.	will
We ——— be able to arrange something for you.	may
He ——— have passed the entrance exam.	must
Why don't you go and ask her if she ——— go with us?	can (will)
We ——— be there in about a half an hour.	will (can)
Some of the students ——— do the assignment without help while others ——— need some assistance.	can; will
——— I borrow your car this afternoon?	May (Can)
You ——— borrow it if you ——— drive.	may; can
He ——— do the work or he ——— fail the exam.	must; will
What time ——— you arrange to be here?	can

14 C

Let me know if you ——— be there by eight o'clock.	can (will)
You ——— be very tired after your long trip.	must
I ——— give you the last chance.	shall (will)
I ——— have made a mistake in my figures.	must
I ——— understand most of it, but you ——— have to explain a few things.	can; will
Let me know if you ——— be able to come.	will
Many questions ——— be answered at the meeting.	will (may)

8 F

He doesn't usually ——— before seven o'clock.

She ——— over there quite often.

If we ——— about seven we will get there on time.

He has ——— all this work for me to do.

I wish you'd tell him about it when he ——— in.

The bus ——— every hour on the hour.

She ——— over here so she could have some peace.

I should ——— over there and see him sometime today.

Close the door when you ———.

I should have ——— there last week.

Bring me something to eat when you ——— back.

Most of the students have ——— home for the holidays.

If you ———, take these with you.

Most of the students ——— before I did.

They have ——— here several times before.

9 A   take, bring

I will ——— the class next semester.

He said he had ——— the books to the library.

Please ——— your books with you.

Some of the students ——— trouble with this assignment,
but I ———n't ——— any.

are having;
have; had

He ——— a hard time learning English.

is having

He ——— many interesting experiences in his life.

has had

She ——— here since early yesterday.

has been

The queen of the ball ——— selected right now.

is being

14 A

modals, present—
can, shall, may, will, must

The wheel ——— turn for the car to go.

must

Ask him if he thinks he ——— do the work.

can

I ——— go if I receive an invitation.

may (can) (will)
(must) (shall)

Let's go to the show; we ——— do the assignment tomorrow.

can

There's an emergency, so I ——— leave for home right away.

must

I ———'t think when you rush me that way.

can

I ——— or ——— not go, depending on the circumstances.

may; may

Why ——— you always interrupt me?

must

I will attempt it, but I ——— fail.

may

How many of you ——— promise to come?

will

He ——— swim very well because he practices every day.

can (must)

I ——— give you my answer tomorrow.

shall (will) (can)

If he said he would come, he ———.

will

I ——— make a decision tomorrow.

may (can) (will)
(must)

We were told to ——— a lunch with us.

The gift ——— me much pleasure.

He asked if he could ——— his sister over.

He is ——— several courses at school.

Mary is ——— the food for our picnic.

He ——— my hand and talked to me.

Several of the men ——— their wives to the meeting.

Are you ——— your wife with you to that meeting?

What did you ——— me?

Who ——— the papers on the table?

Why did you ——— that here with you?

What are you ——— with you when you go?

9 B

What should I ——— on my trip?

He ——— his medicine regularly.

I ——— too many things with me on this trip.

I ——— too many things on my last trip.

How much money did you ——— for the gift?

The doctor said to ——— two pills three times a day.

Be sure and ——— your warm coat tonight.

Where should I ——— these things?

Don't hurry; ——— your time.

He ——— us some lovely gifts from Europe.

Have you ——— your medicine?

We ——— plenty of time to finish the work.	have had
She ———n't ——— as good as she knows how to be.	is; being
It ——— a long time since she ——— here.	has been; has been
They ——— a party when we arrived last night.	were having
He ——— a hard time doing his work.	has had
They ——— trying to reach you for hours.	have been
When we asked about them, we were told that they ——— there earlier but had left.	had been
John ——— several good opportunities for work.	has had
We ——— enough of this foolishness.	have had
It ——— a long time since we've seen him.	has been
There ——— many changes around here since you left.	have been
See if there ——— a mail delivery yet.	has been

13 F

This ——— published before.	has been
They ——— a party tonight.	are having
How many of you ——— here before?	have been
Nearly everyone ——— some problems.	has had
I ——— a cold for over a week.	have had
John ——— many problems this week.	has had
They ——— trouble with their car.	are having
Mr. Smith ——— asked to be the president.	has been
She ——— nothing but trouble with it ever since she bought it.	has had

Rats ——— the plague to the country.

Clouds ——— rain.

She is ——— us some things from Japan.

She ——— several things with her.

9 C

Mr. Johnson wants to ——— all his children over to the show.

The students ——— their books here every day.

He ——— many things with him when he came.

Father ——— the baby from Mother.

Will you ——— out two folders from that file cabinet and ——— them to me immediately?

I ——— some food out of the freezer for our dinner.

She should ——— the pills before going to bed.

——— the cake out of the oven before 3 o'clock.

My faithful dog usually ——— me the newspaper.

Should I ——— this ladder to him?

The carpenter forgot to ——— his tools when he came to work yesterday morning so I ——— his car and ——— them to him.

He always ——— his things with him when he goes.

9 D

The children ——— all their toys to me every day.

Will you ——— the garbage can out to the front, please?

She ——— perfect attendance in that class.   has had

He should ——— there yesterday.   have been

13 D

He ——— very temperamental.   is being

They ——— a special party for her.   are having

He ——— there frequently during the past few weeks.   has been

He ——— a lot of money during his lifetime.   has had

I'm sure you ——— here before.   have been

As long as I can remember, there ——— no one here by   has been
that name.

They ——— that car for a long time.   have had

China ——— several severe earthquakes.   has had

I ——— trouble with my car.   am having

My brother ——— several opportunities to visit Samoa.   has had

Finally, the work ——— completed.   has been

I ——— here for over two years.   have been

They ——— in Italy and France.   have been

It seems like they ——— trouble all their lives.   have had

John and Mary ——— writing to each other for a long time.   have been

13 E

It seems like we ——— here for years.   have been

He ——— many trials in his life.   has had

Who is going to ——— those packages here to the office?

Will you ——— out the two folders from that file cabinet?

Will you ——— him to me as soon as he gets here?

The policeman ——— the burglar in to be questioned after he caught him.

I ——— some food out of the freezer last night.

She always ——— her pills before going to bed.

March always ——— spring rains.

Mother asked me to ——— this ladder out to him.

She ——— the exam and failed it, so she'll ——— another one in a month.

I wasn't sure how long we'd be, so I ——— my lunch.

My grandmother always ——— presents with her wherever she goes and we are always excited about what she ——— us.

9 E

Be sure to ——— a camera with you.

Everyone always ——— his lunch to work.

It may ——— a long time to finish this project.

We were invited to ——— guests.

It ——— a long time to finish.

I'm not going to ——— a camera this time as I ——— one on our last trip and didn't use it.

Spring showers usually ——— many flowers.

He always ——— too much time to work and has no time to play.

Although it ——— much time and effort to do it correctly, it will ——— you the satisfaction of a job well done.

It ——— a long time since it has rained here.   has been

He ——— four cars in the past two years.   has had

We ——— some good times and some bad ones during the past year.   have had

They ———n't ——— any rain there for the past three months.   have; had

They ——— trouble before they came here and ——— a lot of trouble since they arrived.   had had; have had

Many of the students ——— this class before.   have had

She ——— a good time now.   is having

Some of the students ——— here for over two years.   have been

One of them ——— here since 1971.   has been

13 C

It ——— raining for several days now.   has been

Why ———n't they ——— notified?   have; been

One of the boys ——— a party tonight.   is having

We ———n't ——— any rain for a month.   have; had

The dean ——— several of the students meet with him this afternoon.   is having

She ——— as good as she knows how to be.   is being

We could ——— there by now if we had hurried.   have been

——— he ——— the car fixed yet?   Has; had

The car ——— fixed now.   is being

He ——— three accidents this year.   has had

We ——— a party tonight and want you to come.   are having

One of the students ———n't ——— here for several days.   has; been

I'm afraid someone ——— hurt.   has been

——— a warm coat as it might be cold there.

How many of you ——— your lunch with you today?

He ——— the exam last week, but I have to ——— it tomorrow.

9 F

Why don't you ——— your things and leave?

He ——— his friend over to meet us.

She didn't ——— anything with her when she left.

——— me those books from the table over there.

He always ——— his lunch with him when he goes.

Why didn't you ——— the baby over so I could watch him?

If you ——— those things off the desk, ——— them over here
to me.

He ——— in some fresh vegetables from the garden and
——— the meat from the freezer.

Are we supposed to ——— our lunches when we go?

I have ——— all I can from my boss.

She should have ——— her lunch with her.

Are we supposed to ——— our lunches when we come?

She always ——— some presents with her when she goes.

13 A   **be** and *have* **in combinations**
                   as verbs and auxiliaries—
                   has had, has been, had been,
                   is having, are having, am having,
                   was having, were having, had had

They ——— a fight every night.	have had
We ——— another get-together next week.	are having
Why ———n't he ——— the car fixed?	has; had
I think she ——— enough time to finish the test.	has had
She ——— guests for dinner tonight.	is having
They ———n't ——— many opportunities before.	have; had
They ——— a Christmas party.	are having
I ———n't ——— enough to do.	have; had
We ——— always ——— a car.	have; had
She ———n't ——— that very long.	has; had
She ——— a good time when we saw her last.	was having
John ——— an accident.	has had
He said he ———n't ——— enough notice.	has; had
They ——— a test in English today.	are having
Mary ——— never ——— time to do it.	has; had

13 B

We ——— there several times already.	have been
She ——— some trouble with her work in the lab.	is having (has had)
They ——— friends in for dinner tonight.	are having
He ——— good for over a month now; we haven't had any trouble with him at all.	has been

10 A   get, make, do

He barely manages to ——— by in his work.

He doesn't ——— any more than he has to.

That ——— me sick.

She ——— most of her own clothes last year.

He's trying to ——— out of ——— the assignments.

What do you expect to ——— from this class?

He wants to ——— some money this year.

He ——— a lot of friends on his trip.

What do you expect to ——— in this class?

He wants to ——— ahead.

Where can I ——— my paycheck?

He ——— very well in his work.

How much money ——— he ———?

10 B

He always ——— his own breakfast.

Why does he ——— that all the time?

Sometimes he ——— mad at everybody.

It's too far for you to walk; let me ——— it for you.

He always ——— a big fuss about things.

He's afraid he'll ——— fired if he goes.

That ——— three days in a row that he's been late.

You ——— due here an hour ago.   were

Where ——— the children gone and where will they ———   have; be
this evening?

He ——— coming tomorrow and will ——— here for six   is; be;
weeks if we ——— a place for him.   have

You should ——— come to see me immediately.   have

There ——— been no one here by that name for the past   has
two years.

I ——— sure you're right.   am

12 F

She ——— it now, but John will ——— it tomorrow.   has; have

Check these figures and ——— them recorded immediately.   have

One of them ——— a cold and the other ——— out of town.   has; is

Come quickly as John ——— had a bad accident.   has

He is ——— very temperamental.   being

Although half of the apple is bad the other half could ——— be
eaten.

It can't ——— that late! It seems like we've only ——— here   be; been
for a short time.

John said he ——— bringing his friends over as they are ——— is; having
an impromptu party.

Where ——— all the time gone?   has

I can ——— ready in a minute as I only ——— to comb my   be; have
hair.

He said that he was ——— a new secretary.

What has he ——— now?

He never ——— any excuses.

He's always ——— into trouble.

What does he think he's ———?

How much is he ——— each week?

We have ——— several shipments lately.

He ——— a good salary.

10 C

I ——— tired early, so I quit.

What ——— the wheels go around?

She has ——— a lot of money.

He ——— a big raise.

Where did you ——— that?

The early bird ——— the worm.

That should ——— it for now.

He is ——— his best, but he isn't ——— anywhere.

Why don't you ——— some good help?

She always ——— her own bread.

He has ——— into trouble before.

They haven't ——— anything illegal yet.

She has always ——— her own bread.

The neighbors ——— a big fuss about it.

12 D

You should ——— known better than that.	have
They ——— there before I ———.	were; was
How many accidents ——— occurred on this corner?	have
Most of the children ——— hungry and tired.	were (are)
He hasn't ——— an accident yet.	had
Why ——— he done that so often?	has
He should ——— ashamed of himself.	be
I think they ——— carried this too far.	have
Mary ——— late this morning.	was (is)
The candidates ——— all confident they would win.	were
John is ——— a great time swimming.	having
He has ——— a lot of problems with his family.	had
He told me he ———n't been there in years.	had
Why haven't you ——— coming to class?	been

12 E

It can't ——— that bad.	be
What ——— he done this time?	has
The class ——— always prepared last year.	was
He should have ——— here an hour ago.	been
I think he'll ——— here any minute.	be
Mary just phoned and said John ——— had an accident.	had

10 D

We must ——— our work done right away.

He has ——— all he can at present.

He ——— his work well.

What time ——— he usually ——— his work done?

He said he would ——— his work before he left.

He always ——— his work finished on time.

They have ——— many mistakes in the past.

He always ——— his work on time.

I wish he would ——— up his mind about what he will ———.

She always ——— good grades.

When does she ——— her homework?

She ——— herself some new clothes last week.

She was ——— her homework when I called.

10 E

Somehow or other she seems to ——— by.

Singing seems to ——— the day go faster.

Where did you ——— that tool?

He always ——— a good job and ——— good money.

He tried to ——— out of ——— the assignment.

He ——— lots of friends while he was there.

He is ——— a good job, as he is trying to ——— ahead.

He ——— several of them and there are others who ——— some too.	has; have
He ——— to be there on time every day.	has
They ——— gone before we got there.	were (had)
It ——— a good thing I went to see him.	was (is)
How many of you have ——— here before?	been
You can ——— it if you wish.	have
He doesn't ——— much money to spend.	have
Please bring some with you if you ——— any left.	have
Nearly everyone ——— had some problems in his life.	has

12 C

He ——— tried hard to learn English, and ——— still trying hard to learn it.	has; is
——— you been here before?	Have
Where ——— all the children gone?	have
One of the children ——— in the house.	is
Both of the girls ——— there yesterday.	were
Where ——— all the children?	are (were)
At present, everyone ——— well except Mary; she ——— a cold.	is; has
I ———n't had a cold for years.	have
He has ——— many trials in his life.	had
Most of the boys ——— cheerfully done their work.	have
They are ——— trouble with their car.	having
He has ——— asked to be president.	been
They never ——— any trouble while they were there.	had

She always ——— excuses because she ——— so poorly.

That ——— the third time he's ——— that.

He is always ——— into trouble.

10 F

He's always ——— things hard for us.

Why don't you ——— the tickets?

She ——— too many excuses.

He's always ——— things the hard way.

He ——— a lot of money, but it always seemed to ——— away from him.

What has he ——— that has ——— you so mad?

We ——— our best, but we ——— lots of mistakes.

He ——— into trouble when he ——— that before.

I ——— tired when I ——— all those things.

Why didn't you ——— here on time?

11 A   say, tell

He ——— he'd come tomorrow.

I haven't ——— him yet, but plan on it tomorrow.

What do you think he'll ——— when you ——— him?

12 A

be and **have** as either verbs
or auxiliaries—*am, are, is, was,
were, be, been, being, has,
have, had*

He has ——— gone for a long time.   been

We ——— had a hard time getting our work done.   have

The meal ——— eaten quickly.   was

I ——— sure the president is right because he ——— authority.   am; has

We ——— to bring all our books to class every day.   have

We ——— always happy to see him when he comes.   are

There ——— a heavy rainstorm last week.   was

We asked about him, but they said he ——— left.   had

We ——— been unhappy with the results.   had

John hasn't ——— much time to prepare the report.   had

One of the boys ———n't finished yet.   has

If anyone ——— a copy of the report I'd like to see it.   has

Most of the people ——— been here before.   have

There are several people present here who ——— at the   were
dedication last year.

12 B

We have ——— given many instructions.   been

This ——— been published before.   has

He can ——— good if he tries.   be

Please don't ——— so noisy.   be

They ——— coming to see us tonight.   are

He didn't ——— us his plans.

She had already ——— me the news.

They didn't ——— anything about their plans.

John ——— he had been too busy to do it.

He ——— his wife that he would be late for dinner.

You really should ——— the truth about it.

He ——— exactly what he thought about the project.

He ——— us that he didn't like the plan.

She is ——— all kinds of things about you.

I ——— him it wasn't nice to ——— things like that.

11 B

She ——— us, and I'm sure she is going to ——— everyone.

He didn't ——— why he was going.

She's been ——— a lot of things about you.

He ——— he would ——— us before he ——— anyone else.

She ——— her friend had ——— her about the announcement.

He ——— he had enjoyed his trip immensely.

He ——— he was ——— the truth.

Mary ——— the children a story.

Most of his friends ——— him he is very handsome.

I wouldn't ——— anything about it if I were you.

All of the girls ——— finished their work.   have

Why ———n't someone mended the fence?   has

They ——— a wonderful family.   have

One of the books ——— some pages missing.   has

One of you ——— to do the work.   has

11 G

She ——— always succeeded in everything.   has

He ——— always ——— a lot of money.   has; had

They ——— a lot of money left to them.   had

I ——— to go now.   have

They ——— three children before they left here.   had

He ——— ten dollars but he ——— spent it all.   had; has

He ——— worked here for the past two years.   has

Where ——— she been for the past hour?   has

What does that ——— to do with the subject?   have

It ——— taken us a long time to get here.   has

They have ——— some interesting experiences.   had

Why ——— she come?   has

We ——— three choices.   have

11 C

He ——— he hadn't done it, but she ——— everyone he had.

He didn't ——— why he had already ——— most of his friends.

She has been ——— that for years.

He has ——— that story a dozen times.

She didn't ——— when she would be ready to ———
us her plans.

Mary ——— me she wouldn't do it again.

Why didn't she ——— that before?

You really should have ——— them the truth.

He didn't ——— when he would be going.

I wonder why they didn't ——— anything about it to me?

I ——— exactly what I meant.

I didn't think she would ——— on me.

11 D

Mr. Jones ——— that he thought his wife had ——— me about it.

Yesterday they ——— the children the truth.

He was so astonished he couldn't ——— anything.

She ——— that she had ——— you everything.

She is ——— everybody that you ——— that.

I'm going to walk right up and ——— what I think.

She hasn't ——— she would go, but she hasn't ——— she
wouldn't either.

We ——— many strange experiences on our trip.	had
He hasn't ——— many opportunities to speak English in the past.	had
We ——— several choices at this time.	have
He ——— his writings published.	had
What ——— you done with the tickets?	have
The work ——— never been completed.	has
They ——— been here for a long time.	have
He ——— a great interest in the program.	has
I ——— several copies so you may have one.	have
She ——— great talent.	has

11 F

He has ——— many interesting experiences in his life.	had
She ——— gone there several times.	has
He ———n't been here since yesterday.	has
We ——— finished long before the time was up.	had
He asked me if I ——— any money.	had
Why ——— you come to see me?	have
It ———n't rained here for a long time.	has
We ——— had lots of trouble.	have
I ——— an opportunity to go to school next year.	have
One of the boys ——— a cold and can't come.	has

He ——— that, didn't he?

Don't ——— anything about what he just ——— you.

She ——— that he always does that.

11 E

He ——— that the children had asked him to ——— them a story.

I didn't think she ——— the word correctly, so I looked it up.

She ——— me not to ——— anyone else, and I ——— I wouldn't.

I wish they'd ——— something about it.

I don't think he'll ever ——— that story again.

He ——— me his secret, but I can't ——— anything else.

Why doesn't she ——— something in English?

He ——— something, but I'm sure he didn't ——— the truth.

He hasn't ——— anything about that for years.

Everyone is ——— something different about it.

11 F

I didn't ——— him that she had already ——— me the news.

He didn't ——— when he expected to go to California.

She just ——— that so people will listen to her.

He ——— that story to anyone who will listen; I think he's ——— it a dozen times.

He didn't ——— us what he was going to ——— at the meeting.

99

11 D

How many times ——— he told you about it?	has
He ——— done that several times.	has
She ——— her turn last week.	had
He has ——— several chances.	had
How many times ——— you told her about it?	have
They might ——— been there before.	have
Mary ——— broken her watch before she left.	had
He couldn't ——— done it.	have
How many times ——— you been there?	have
He ——— studied English before he came here.	had
We have ——— several chances to go.	had
Who ——— the time?	has
Who could ——— done that?	have
John ——— to go now.	has
He has done more than he should ——— done.	have

11 E

What ——— you done with my book?	have
He ——— finished his work before he came.	had
I ——— to finish my work before I can go.	have
She ——— a new dress for the party tonight.	has
What ——— he done with my book?	has

I'm not sure that I ——— you what he ———.

He couldn't have ——— them anything about it.

He ——— he thought that was the way it happened.

People are ——— they think you know something about it.

He has ——— that before, and I've ——— him so.

12 A   want, need

She ——— her job here and doesn't ——— to leave it.

He ——— to buy a new car although he doesn't need one.

Does she ——— to be a teacher?

Students ——— to register before school starts.

If you ——— to see him you'll ——— to make an appointment.

If everyone comes you'll ——— more chairs.

How many textbooks will we ——— for that course?

Bring a coat if you think you'll ——— one.

Everyone ——— to go when they heard about it.

Bring only what you ——— as there is very little room.

What do I ——— to make a cake?

Bring it if you ——— to, but I don't think you'll ——— it.

Some of them are ——— trouble with it.   having

Have you ——— any trouble with it?   had

Why don't you ——— someone fix it who knows how?   have

They ——— had that car for a long time.   have

He ——— a good job last year.   had

Why doesn't he ——— someone fix it who knows how?   have

Mary has ——— several chances to go to Japan.   had

He's ——— a hard time learning English.   having

11 C

Mary never ——— time to do it.   has

If I ——— more time I'd do it myself.   had

He often ——— friends in for dinner.   has

They usually ——— a wonderful time.   have

He is ——— a lot of trouble.   having

Where ——— all the time gone?   has

I ——— seen that man before.   have

He ———n't seen her for a long time.   has

Where ——— all the people gone?   have

I ——— always had to hurry to get there on time.   have

She could ——— gone if she ——— wanted to.   have; had

Are they ——— friends in tonight?   having

They ——— a good time at the party.   had

Everyone ——— some problems.   has

12 B

We ――― chicken for dinner tomorrow.

You ――― a haircut.

The dean said he ――― to see you.

This lawn ――― mowing.

He ――― to go to the dentist as he has a toothache.

She ――― us to write an essay for homework.

He ――― help! He's drowning.

He ――― a hamburger for lunch.

When she grows up, she ――― to be just like her mother.

We ――― to store food and water in case of an emergency.

What do I ――― to do to help you?

His mother ――― her son to get a college education.

This house ――― to be painted.

The teacher ――― all the students to be present at the lecture.

He ――― to marry someone like his mother.

12 C

What do I ――― to do to help you?

What do you ――― to eat tonight?

What will I ――― for the trip?

What do you ――― to do with your life?

Invite anyone you ――― to the party.

11 A

review of *have—*
have, has had

He ———n't had a chance to do much about it.	has
One of the girls ——— finished the test already.	has
——— anyone seen my paper? I ——— it a short while ago.	Has; had
Where ——— everyone gone?	has
There ———n't been anyone around for a long time.	has
One of the boys is ——— a party tonight.	having
Which of you ——— the assignment for tonight?	has
I ——— had many different thoughts about the matter.	have
Mr. Jones could ——— gone to Suva.	have
We ———n't been anywhere for a long time.	have
He must ——— seen it somewhere.	have
If he ———n't seen it who ———?	has; has
They were ——— some trouble with their car, so I helped them.	having

11 B

One of the students ——— two copies of the assignments so he gave me one.	had
He could ——— finished if he ——— tried.	have; had
I'm ——— trouble with my boat motor.	having
She has ——— nothing but trouble with it ever since she bought it.	had
He is ——— his tooth pulled this afternoon.	having
One of them ——— a cold.	has

The student ——— to take eighteen hours although he only ——— to take twelve.

Parents usually ——— the best for their children.

He is overweight because he eats what he ——— instead of what he ———.

Students ——— a library clearance before they receive their grades.

He ——— to take his vacation in July.

Bring everything you'll ——— because you won't be able to buy anything there.

What do you ——— for Christmas?

He needs help but doesn't ——— to ask for it.

12 D

If you ——— the job you'll ——— to impress the manager.

When do you ——— me to come?

He said he would call if he ——— anything.

She makes enough money to buy everything she ———, but not everything she often ———.

The boys are trapped on the ledge and ——— help to get down.

Some day I ——— to travel and see the world, and I ——— to do it before I'm too old to enjoy it.

To make a good salad one ——— fresh produce.

You will ——— to look after your sister while I'm gone.

If he could have everything he ———, he thinks he would be happy.

He can't have ——— that many failures.   had

You really should ——— your teeth fixed.   have

He may ——— some trouble with the immigration office   have;
as he has ——— some in the past.   had

Why hasn't anyone ——— this fixed?   had

John might ——— it if Mary doesn't.   have

They were ——— a hard time when I left.   having

He might be ——— a party tonight.   having

The library might ——— the books you want.   have

10 F

We really haven't ——— a lot of fun here.   had

I heard that Mary is ——— a party tonight.   having

She's ——— a cold for a week.   had

I've ——— that coat for a long time and wish I could ———   had; have
a new one.

All the students are ——— trouble with that problem.   having

Bring it over if you're ——— trouble so I can ——— a look   having; have
at it.

John may ——— trouble starting the car as I have often   have;
——— problems starting it.   had

His parents are ——— trouble again.   having

They have never ——— any trouble with it before.   had

He should ——— my book as I loaned it to him last week.   have

She has ——— a lot of colds this year.   had

They're ——— several students come over tonight.   having

Be sure and buy everything we'll ——— to make pizza.

He should see a doctor as he ——— help.

He just ——— some attention, so he's making a scene.

12 E

The trees ——— watering today.

The whole country ——— rain.

I don't ——— it to rain because we're having a picnic.

The children ——— some new clothes for the winter.

He ——— you to come and see him.

He's having a lot of trouble and ——— help.

He ——— many things, but ——— only a few.

He said he ——— to be my friend.

Bring only the things you will ——— as we haven't much room.

He is ——— by the police.

What does one ——— to do to join the club?

Where were you when I ——— your help?

He ——— fried chicken.

I ——— some help or I won't get my work done.

10 D

We're ——— a late lunch.	having
She has ——— a hard time since she came here.	had
She is ——— some trouble with her assignments.	having
Mary might ——— your textbook.	have
I haven't ——— so much fun in years.	had
You haven't ——— enough practice.	had
His parents were ——— to send him money.	having
We should ——— time to stop by the library.	have
They have ——— a long time to think about it.	had
She's ——— some friends in tonight.	having
One of the contestants has ——— to withdraw.	had
When will you be ——— a party again?	having
I wish I could ——— a trip abroad while John wishes he could ——— a new car.	have; have
We're ——— so much fun I don't want to leave.	having

10 E

He must ——— completed his work by now.	have
He says he hasn't ——— enough time to do it.	had
You should ——— known that.	have
We were ——— a good time until the neighbors complained.	having
You really should ——— more money than that.	have
She hasn't ——— that very long.	had

12 F

I ——— to go, but I ——— to save my money for next year's tuition.

How fast do you ——— to run to make the team?

I ——— to go to the party, but I wasn't invited.

Everyone ——— to help although we only ——— two people.

She ——— to buy something, but she ——— to go to the bank first.

He ——— to leave on Monday to get there on time.

She ——— fifteen dollars to buy the things she ———.

Although I have everything I ———, I ——— a few luxuries too.

What do you ——— me to bring you?

They ——— ten thousand dollars to finish the project.

13 A   **want, like**

John ——— Mary; in fact, he ——— to marry her.

What would you ——— for dinner?

He ——— to do the right thing.

He ——— football and soccer.

Why hasn't he ――― the car fixed?   had

She may ――― a cold.   have

They haven't ――― a fight for a long time.   had

They have ――― time to finish the test.   had

John and Mary have ――― many interesting experiences.   had

He said I could ――― it if I wanted it.   have

10 C

Why hasn't he ――― notice of the meeting?   had

They could ――― a good time if they'd go.   have

They are ――― a meeting in the library.   having

I am ――― a few friends in for dinner.   having

He has ――― several chances to go abroad.   had

He could ――― some trouble with the car.   have

He is ――― trouble with his homework.   having

He might ――― it. Have you asked him about it?   have

He had ――― some trouble with the group before that.   had

John is ――― fun swimming in the surf.   having

She hasn't ――― any trouble for a long time.   had

Mary might ――― a cold, although she hasn't ――― one for   have; had
a long time.

I heard that they were ――― some trouble.   having

How much trouble have they ――― recently?   had

When do you ——— to eat?

He ——— to read poetry.

I don't ——— bananas.

What would you ——— to eat?

He says he doesn't ——— to go.

What would they ——— me to bring?

Bring whatever you ——— to.

Most of the students ——— their teachers.

What do you ——— me to bring to the picnic?

What do you ——— to eat?

13 B

Do you ——— to serve dinner now?

Bring whatever you'd ——— to.

He ——— her when he first met her.

She doesn't ——— my work.

He said he ——— to go to Europe last year.

The children ——— their new toys.

He ——— to see you before you leave.

If you don't ——— to go, say so.

What do you ——— out of life?

Do you really ——— an education?

Do you really ——— to study?

They may ——— several children by now.   have

Mary has never ——— time to do it for me.   had

They are ——— a test in English today.   having

They haven't ——— many opportunities before.   had

She is ——— guests for dinner tonight.   having

He said he hadn't ——— enough notice.   had

They aren't ——— a Christmas party this year.   having

I think she has ——— enough time to finish the test.   had

She can ——— them if she wants them.   have

We're ——— another party next week.   having

He will ——— some of them made for me.   have

They have ——— a fight every night.   had

10 B

He has ——— a hard time in school.   had

They are ——— a party tonight and want to know if you   having;
have ——— an invitation.   had

We were ——— trouble with the generator, but it has been   having
fixed.

He has ——— several cars in the past two years.   had

He can ——— some of them if he wants them.   have

We have always ——— a car.   had

I haven't ——— enough to do this past week.   had

They should ——— a copy of it.   have

I ――― to watch movies.

Would you ――― a ride?

He ――― to begin again.

I have ――― one of them for years.

13 C

She called and said she ――― to see you tomorrow.

I would ――― to make an appointment for tomorrow.

Does your boss ――― you to go?

A baby ――― lots of attention.

I'm not really sure what I'd ――― to do.

I ――― to go to the beach, but I'll have to complete
this assignment first.

She's studying hard because she ――― to pass the test.

What does he ――― me to do?

Bring whatever you ――― to bring.

He said he'd ――― to bring ice cream.

She said she ――― it well enough to buy it.

What she ――― to do and what she has to do are two
different things.

She's studying hard because she'd ――― to pass the test.

I ――― to go, but I didn't have time.

She would have ――― to have gone, but she couldn't
find the time.

9 F

Bring all the things you ――― finished with you.	have
Ask him if he ――― completed the report.	has
He ――― worked on it in Tonga and ――― also worked on it since he came here.	had; has
The school board ――― given us permission to have a field trip.	has (had)
He ――― made several canoes.	has
My father ――― often brought me to school.	has
Most of the things ――― been sold already.	have
Her friends ――― assisted her a great deal.	have
My friend ――― changed his mind about going with us.	has
Many of the things ――― been sold before we arrived.	had
John ――― changed his mind a dozen times.	has
He ――― studied English before he took my class.	had
He ――― hoped they would accept him, but they didn't.	had
All our things ――― been in storage for a long time.	have

10 A   **verb *have* with auxiliaries and modals—*have, has, had***

She hasn't ――― that very long.	had
She was ――― a good time when we saw her last.	having
John has ――― an accident.	had

13 D

I'd ——— to go; however, I can't

I've always ——— to read that book.

There are a lot of students who ——— to see you.

Most of the students ——— sports.

Would you ——— to take charge?

What would you ——— to do tomorrow?

He ——— to work.

Most people ——— to succeed in life.

He ——— to borrow the car tomorrow.

He ——— to see you about a loan.

Where would you ——— me to put this?

Why don't you ——— her?

He ——— us to be there on time tomorrow; in fact, he'd ——— us to be there by three o'clock.

How many of you ——— this plan?

13 E

He thought he'd ——— to see the film, but he ——— to read the book first.

How do you ——— my new dress?

I've always ——— one like it.

I ——— to travel and ——— to visit Japan some day.

He ——— to read the book because he ——— the film.

No one ——— turned in his paper yet.	has
One of the boys ——— gone to every game the team ——— played this year.	has; has
——— you driven a car before you came to America?	Had
If you ———n't turned in your paper you'd better hurry and get it in.	have

9 E

If your father ———n't been there he should go.	has
——— you been studying English long?	Have
The postman ——— been here and left.	has
Where ——— you put your papers?	have
He ———n't read the assignment yet.	has
He ——— already driven my car before I gave him permission to.	had
How many times ——— you attended class?	have
I ———n't ever traveled there.	have
She ———n't filled out the form yet.	has
He ——— taken the exam before the others did.	had
John ——— just received a package from home.	has
——— it started to rain before you arrived?	Had
My grandmother ——— lived here all her life.	has
We ——— known that man for years.	have
My brother ——— already written his report.	has

Do you ——— playing football?

Which game do you ——— to play tonight?

He thought he ——— to play on the team, but he's changed his mind.

Most students ——— sports.

He gets along well with everyone as he ——— people.

I ——— to go to the beach, but it looks like I won't get what I ——— as long as it's raining.

13 F

She ——— pancakes and eats them for breakfast every day.

He ——— to go home.

What do you ——— to do tomorrow?

When would you ——— to go?

I think he ——— to see you.

He said he ——— to see a movie.

Do you really ——— to eat raw fish?

I don't even ——— to taste it.

He ——— to listen to classical music.

Where do you ——— to sit at the concert?

Who ——— to go with me?

He'd ——— to go swimming.

He ——— fifty dollars for his work.

Why do you ——— to go?

Either John or Mary ——— already completed the work before I arrived.

had

He ——— been a teacher for years.

has

One of the boys ——— fallen overboard.

has

They ——— faced many problems but ——— solved them all.

have; have

Both John and Mary ——— completed their work.

have

Why ——— you done it this way?

have

We ——— always tried to satisfy our customers.

have

Most of the meal ——— been eaten before we arrived.

had

Several of them ——— already finished before the rest started.

had

Bring me all the things Mary ——— done so far.

has

Most of the students ——— taken English in their own countries.

have

9 D

——— you ever driven a car before?

Have

——— she ever met him before the party?

Had

It ——— begun to rain before I left the house.

had

What did he say after he ——— read the letter?

had

He ——— waited for a long time to come here.

has

Mary told me she ——— received a letter from her aunt.

had

He ——— traveled all through the Far East.

has

The whole class ——— read the text beforehand.

had

I ———n't met your sister yet.

have

What ——— you eaten today?

have

14 A   like, want, need

I would ——— to see you dance at the Polynesian Cultural Center.

His mother ——— her son to get a college education.

The house ——— to be painted.

He ——— to go to the concert.

Would you ——— some envelopes? I have more than I ———.

When she grows up she ——— to be just like her mother.

I would ——— a roast beef sandwich, please.

We ——— more money to survive.

I ——— more time to get this finished.

He ——— chicken for dinner tomorrow.

We ——— to store food in case of famine.

We ——— to hurry because we ——— to go to the beach.

You ——— more help than I can give you.

14 B

He's ill and ——— to see the doctor.

Did he ——— his present?

Why doesn't he ——— to help us?

He ——— to study even if he doesn't ——— to.

We ——— to leave by ten if we expect to get there on time.

Where do you ——— to go on your vacation?

9 B

She ――― spoken to me twice.	has
We ―――n't seen her around for a long time.	have
I ――― been here several times.	have
They ――― traveled extensively.	have
Where ――― everyone gone?	has
Some students ――― already done all the assignments, so will have lots of free time.	have
One of the students ――― finished the first part of the assignment before the class started.	had
――― you heard the good news?	Have
Someone ――― helped them before they came here.	had
Half of the class members ――― finished that assignment.	have
Everyone ――― finished, so all of you may go home.	has
What ――― you eaten for breakfast before you got sick?	had
Why ―――n't you written your mother?	have
Why ―――n't you written to your sister before the holidays?	had
Half of the class ――― finished the first part of the assignment.	has

9 C

He ――― spoken to the girl several times.	has
The two boys ――― been here for a long time.	have
He could have come if he ――― wanted to.	had

John ——— to sing when Mary plays the piano.

They ——— ten thousand dollars before they can start to build their new house.

When do you ——— to go away?

The plants ——— water; they are wilting.

What would you ——— to bring for the picnic?

I'd ——— to leave now as I ——— to get home before dark.

Who do you ——— to invite?

14 C

He said he'd ——— to leave early.

Why does he ——— to leave early? He really doesn't ——— to.

Bring everything you'll ——— on the trip.

He ——— to visit his friends when he has free time.

Bring what you ——— because it's pot luck.

How long do you ——— to stay?

If possible, he would ——— to see you tomorrow.

What do you ——— for your journey?

You will ——— some eggs to make custard.

Everyone ——— to be happy.

You'll ——— a ticket to get in.

I think he would ——— to come too.

Although he ——— to come he couldn't.

He doesn't ——— to talk about it.

All of the students ――― to take English until they meet the requirements.   have

Either Mary or John ――― my English book last.   had

9 A   auxiliary *have—*
                    have, has, had

He ―――n't spoken to me for a long time.   has

Why ――― you brought them to me?   have

He ――― been accustomed to luxuries before he came here.   had

Mary ――― never taken time to do it before we came.   had

Jane ――― been ill for the past week.   has

I ―――n't attended class all week.   have

One of the boys ――― broken his leg.   has

John and Bill ――― finished the work before I came in.   had

Some of the boys ――― been hurt.   have

Either John or his father ――― come to see me every day during the past week.   has

Most of them ――― brought their things with them.   have

When we got there we found that one of the students ――― left his ticket home.   had

Mary, John, and George ――― all read the book before the class.   had

The students ――― come to wish you well in your new undertaking.   have

How many of you ――― read this book before?   have

14 D

How many times do I —— to tell you?

Every living thing —— water.

He really —— to see a doctor even though he doesn't —— to.

I would —— to go with you.

He said he —— to thank you for your gift.

Everyone —— a friend.

Most people would —— more money than they have.

Bring her if you —— to.

He —— a job but doesn't —— that one.

Why don't you —— her?

Do whatever you —— to about it.

He'd —— a better job.

Do whatever you'd —— about it.

14 E

The dog —— a bath; he smells!

He —— to play football and —— to be on the team.

What would you —— to do tomorrow? Most of us —— to go to the beach.

He —— some help or he won't get his work done.

What ――― the most value in your life?   has

Each of us ――― his own opinion.   has

We ――― a wonderful time yesterday.   had

I ――― a complete set now.   have

Where ――― all the time gone?   has

It ――― three parts and needs another one.   has

The class ――― a plan.   has

Half of the apple ――― brown spots on it now.   has

I ――― a bad dream.   had

Half of the apples ――― spots on them now.   have

8 F

The group ―――n't any time to wait for her.   has

John ――― a textbook, but he lost it.   had

Most of us ――― plans for the future, but we ―――n't done   have; have
anything about them.

The members of the group ――― their tickets already.   have

Everyone ――― a great time at the party last night.   had

――― the mailman come yet? I ――― a letter that must be   Has; have
mailed.

Mary ――― the measles so will miss two weeks of school.   has

Every semester many of the students ――― problems with   have
English.

Some of the students ――― problems before they came.   had

When do you ――― time to see me?   have

She always ――― enough time to do the things she wants to do.   has

What do I ——— to do to join the club? I ——— to join.

What would you ——— for dinner tonight?

John ——— a hot dog while Mary ——— a hamburger.

What do we really ——— to take with us? I don't ——— to take anything we don't ——— to take.

What do you ——— to do tomorrow?

14 F

He's always happy because he ——— everyone.

How much money do you think he ——— to just get by?

He is ——— by the police.

I'd ——— to do something that I really ——— to do for a change instead of something I really ——— to do.

Where were you when I ——— you to help me?

I'd ——— to go to the dance, and Mary ——— to go too.

Bring anything you'd ———.

I ——— movies, don't you?

I don't ——— to ride, I ——— to ride.

I ——— to go too, but I just couldn't make it.

I ——— to study, or I'll fail the test.

8 D

——— he any experience in that field?	Has
She ——— several of them at home now.	has
What do you ——— there?	have
She ——— several children before she went to school.	had
My car ——— a flat tire on the trip.	had
He should ——— some ideas.	have
We ———n't time to go now.	have
This door ——— a broken lock.	has
Come down when you ——— time.	have
One of the boys ——— a broken leg and couldn't go.	had
Everyone ——— his own problems.	has
At times, everybody ——— ideas.	has
Someone ——— the book before I did.	had
All of the boys ——— some money, so we won't have any problems.	have
Anyone ——— a chance to win, but only one boy won.	had

8 E

All of the boys ——— books.	have
His comments ——— a big effect on the decision.	had
One of the boys ——— a car we can use.	has
Some people ——— many problems.	have
Which of the boys ——— the accident?	had

15 A look, watch, see

He never ——— television.

Why do you want to ——— that program?

I can't ——— from here.

When do you think you will ——— him again?

He always ——— at the audience when he performs.

He ——— the performance last night.

I haven't ——— my brother for years.

——— at those boys over there playing basketball.

He tried to ——— three different games at the same time.

What do you ——— in him anyway?

I'll ——— for it tomorrow.

——— those boys over there playing basketball?

He ——— TV every night; I don't know what he ——— in it.

He never ——— at her or spoke to her all evening.

15 B

He sat and ——— at her picture for hours.

He ——— over this way, but I don't think he ——— me.

She always ——— television.

The average child in America ——— TV at least four
hours a day.

He didn't ——— everything he wanted to at the fair.

Let's ——— the next race.

I ——— several new books at home.   have

They ———n't enough time now to finish their work.   have

Some of the students always ——— lots of problems.   have

8 C

Half of the picture ——— mud on it; we'd better clean it up.   has

If I ——— the choice, I'd go in a minute.   had

If he ——— a chance, he'll go.   has

How many ——— books and can start now?   have

One of the students ——— a cold and can't come.   has

What ——— that to do with it?   has (had)

Half of the pictures ——— mud on them and need cleaning.   have

It ——— a pleasant smell; you'll probably like it.   has

Some of the students ——— colds and can't come.   have

One of the students ——— a cold and couldn't come.   had

He ——— better study or he'll fail the course.   had

Neither Mary nor her mother ——— time to do it before   has
morning.

I didn't like it because it ——— an unpleasant odor.   had

Which of these ——— the best tone?   has

Both of them ——— a good tone.   have

Let's wait a while and ——— if anything happens.

He's ——— at the report now.

She ——— like her mother.

He doesn't want to ——— that program, but wants to ——— another one.

Before crossing the street one should ——— out for cars by first ——— one way and then the other.

From where we stood, we couldn't ——— the performance.

15 C

How many of the movies in the series have you ———?

Do you like to ——— the people when they perform?

He likes to ——— at picture books.

Bring the baby over, I'll ——— her for you.

How many of them can you ——— from here?

I'd like to ——— the performance; let's stay and ——— it.

Which kind of TV shows do you usually ———?

After you've ——— the program, I'd like your opinion of it.

We ——— the game for about an hour and then left.

After he had ——— over the field he decided to stay and ——— the game.

Did you ——— the game last week?

I spent all day long yesterday ——— for it.

He always ——— the games on Monday nights.

Several of the students ――― their work with them.   have

One of the students ――― a cold last week.   had

Half of this apple ――― spots on it.   has

We ――― to go and see the doctor this afternoon.   have

Half of these apples ――― spots on them.   have

Half of the work ――― errors in it.   has (had)

This semester some of the students on campus ――― cars.   have

One of them ―――n't a car now.   has

If you ――― time, come and see me.   have

We ――― to finish our work before we left.   had

8 B

This vase ――― a blemish and needs to be fixed.   has

It ――― a blemish so they sold it at half price.   had

He ―――n't any left when we arrived.   had

We ――― lots of time to finish our work before the period ended.   had

They ――― their books now and can start the lesson.   have

It ――― a blemish so they should sell it at half price.   has

Half of the rice ――― weevils in it.   has (had)

I ――― a headache and think I'll go and lie down.   have

Bring me some apples if you ――― any.   have

Half of these apples ――― worms in them.   have

He ――― five As and one B.   has (had)

She ――― many problems with her house before she moved.   had

15 D

I'll ——— the baby while you ——— to the other things.

I ——— the accident happen and stayed until help arrived.

Why doesn't he ——— where he is going? He could have ——— that car.

Everyone doesn't ——— things the same way.

I'd ——— my language if I were you.

He's ——— this way; let's hope he——— us.

He asked to ——— over his homework to ——— if he had done it correctly.

Let's wait and ——— what happens when they ——— what he's done to the house.

He ——— like he's mad at what he ———.

15 E

He ——— at her but didn't speak.

He's been ——— her very closely all evening.

It didn't ——— like he was going to make it,

He didn't ——— anything in it for him, so he left.

She's ——— all over for you.

7 G

You should try and ––– on time tomorrow.	be
How long have you ––– here?	been
One of the boys ––– hurt yesterday.	was
He ––– going to try again tomorrow.	is
They ––– usually happy when they ––– here during the holidays last year.	were; were
He is ––– scolded by the instructor.	being
Some of these apples ––– bad.	are
Which of the girls over there ––– your friend?	is
When ––– he here last?	was
I saw several of the students who ––– waiting for the grades to ––– posted.	were; be
Which dessert ––– the best?	is
They had ––– in Europe before they ––– here last year.	been; were

8 A   verb *have—*
have, has, had

He ––– several opportunities to perform while he was there.	had
She ––– lots of friends.	has
How many problems do you ––– to finish?	have
Her mother ––– several new books.	has
He ––– a cold, but he is better now.	had

You stay and ——— the game and I'll ——— if I can locate her.

All the travelers were ——— for their luggage as they couldn't ——— it on the baggage cart.

She loves to ——— TV; she ——— at that screen all day.

She doesn't ——— very well today. Has she been sick?

I ——— her yesterday, and she ——— better than she did then.

He's been ——— that show for an hour.

15 F

Why don't you come over to my house and ——— TV with me?

I have something in my eye and can't ——— very well.

I wish he'd ——— at me once in a while; I really don't ——— what he ——— in her.

I want to ——— that new play everyone's talking about.

She didn't ——— at all startled when she saw him here.

Let's ——— and ——— what happens.

I wish you'd ——— over these plans and ——— what's wrong with them.

I told her she'd better ——— sharp and ——— her actions or she'd be in trouble.

He wants to ——— the ball game so he'll ——— it on TV.

He ——— afraid he will ——— late for the meeting.   is; be

They ——— taken yesterday while we ——— gone.   were; were

He has ——— my best friend for years.   been

He is ——— sought by the police.   being

Where ——— he when I needed him?   was

7 F

All of the team members ——— hurt during the game.   were

He has ——— gone a long time.   been

He ——— frequently absent from class.   is

One of the apples ——— bad.   was (is)

John, with his father, ——— present at the meeting.   was

Everyone but Mary ——— there.   was

The news ——— soon forgotten.   was

All of the class members except Mary ——— there.   were

There ——— too many errors on the paper, so John ———   were; was
told to rewrite it.

Where ——— John when it happened?   was

He should ——— here now.   be

There ——— a nice restaurant near here.   is

Have you ——— here before?   been

The boys ——— scolded for their actions.   were

16 A   listen, hear

You'll have to ——— carefully to ——— what he says.

I was sitting in the back and couldn't ——— what was said.

I have to ——— to her every time she complains.

Why didn't you ——— to what he said the first time?

She thought she ——— him talking.

I wouldn't ——— if I were you, as you won't ———
anything good.

I ——— her the first time.

If you don't ———, you won't ——— the directions.

Why didn't you ——— to what he said the first time?

Turn up the radio so I can ——— it.

Turn on the TV; I want to ——— the news.

Turn on the TV; I want to ——— to the news.

16 B

Let's ——— to the concert tonight, but let's go early as
you can't ——— in the back of the hall.

I didn't ——— her say that, but I really didn't ———
very closely.

Turn on the TV; let's ——— to the 5 o'clock news.

Did you ——— anything interesting at the meeting?

It seems to me he can ——— when he wants to.

He told me about it after he ——— it.

7 D

Everyone ——— happy about the party.	was
Either his friends or John ——— going to call on you.	is
Try and ——— on time for a change.	be
One of the girls ——— going to ——— the queen.	is; be
He would have ——— on time if they hadn't come.	been
Some of the books ——— missing yesterday.	were
He ——— selected by the committee.	was
Where have you ——— during the last hour?	been
Most of the students ——— surprised although they shouldn't have ———.	were; been
She ——— on her way to town when she ——— stopped by her friend.	was; was
He should ——— here by now.	be
Which one of the books ——— yours?	is

7 E

All of the students ——— present, but one of them ——— late.	were; was
We have ——— happy here.	been
Sometimes she ——— lonesome.	is
She has ——— late several times.	been
They should ——— here any minute now.	be
What ——— your opinion?	is
I must ——— there tomorrow.	be

Be quiet! We're ——— to the news.

Although he ——— closely, he had trouble ——— the speaker because of the surrounding noise.

That's the first time I've ever ——— that.

Why aren't you ——— to the teacher?

If the children want to ——— the story, they will have to sit quietly on the floor.

If the children want to ——— to the story, they will have to sit quietly on the floor.

16 C

You will have to ——— very carefully or you won't be able to ——— the speaker.

She said she was ———, but she didn't ——— the announcement.

He won't ——— to anyone but his mother.

I wonder why he didn't ——— to you.

He said he only came because he wanted to ——— the main speaker.

I wish I hadn't ——— to him and ——— all the bad news.

He only ——— to one side of the proposition; he should really ——— the other side too.

He said he was tired of ——— to all that chatter, so he went for a walk so he didn't have to ——— it.

I think I'll relax and ——— to the radio for a while.

Oh, I ——— that a long time ago.

I don't repeat everything I ———.

It ——— often difficult to do what is right.   is

The meal ——— prepared quickly last night.   was

We ——— there for several hours.   were

We ——— warned not to go any further.   were

7 C

The table's surface ——— very smooth.   is

One of the boys ——— late last night.   was

The weather ——— better today than it ——— yesterday.   is; was

Where have you ———?   been

Where can he ———?   be

He ——— singing on the program tomorrow.   is

He will ——— here in an hour.   be

He ——— thankful for the food.   was (is)

If we don't hurry, we'll ——— late for the party.   be

He hasn't ——— here very often.   been

It seems like we ——— always late.   are

One of the girls ——— injured by a fall.   was

Both of them ——— present at the meeting.   were

Where can that ——— found?   be

16 D

Speak louder so I can ——— you.

He only ——— to your side of the argument.

He tried to ——— to everyone at once; consequently, he didn't ——— anything that made sense.

Why doesn't the chairman tell them to be quiet and ———?

He tried to ——— what was being said, but it was impossible because of the noise.

No one was ——— to anything anybody else was saying.

Although he doesn't ——— a word I say, I think he understands.

I ——— that too, but I refuse to believe it. I don't like ——— to gossip.

I really didn't ——— that announcement, but, you know, I really wasn't ——— very closely.

Where did you ——— that piece of news?

I ——— very carefully, but I didn't ——— anything about it.

16 E

It seems to me that she only ——— what she wants to ———.

He should have ——— carefully to the instructions, and he might have ——— how to put it together.

Why don't we go and ——— to the concert?

I don't think we can ——— in that part of the room, even if we ——— carefully.

139

He ——— unable to come, but he will send a substitute.	is
She wanted to help but she ———n't prepared.	was
I don't think I need to worry about it; however, it could ——— important.	be
He has ——— trying very hard to do what ——— right.	been; is
It could have ——— a disaster but everything turned out all right.	been
Everything would have ——— wonderful if you had ——— there.	been; been
They ———n't there.	were (are)
He ——— overjoyed with the results.	was (is)
Here ——— the results of the test.	are
Where have you ———?	been

7 B

He has ——— here since three o'clock.	been
Everyone ——— given a special assignment.	was
We were happy to ——— of assistance.	be
Where ——— you when he arrived?	were
It will soon ——— three hours since he arrived.	be
Their tasks ——— all finished on time.	were (are)
Only one of the jobs ——— left to do.	was
They have ——— happy with their work.	been
He ——— being considered for an important position.	is
I ——— tired of hearing excuses every day.	am
She has ——— careful in her work.	been

Most of the students have ——— the news.

He was ——— to some music when I saw him last.

He brought his radio so we could ——— to the broadcast,
but we couldn't ——— it very well as it was noisy on
the beach.

Why don't we go and ——— the concert?

If you had ——— carefully, you would have ——— what he
said.

What was it you ———?

16 F

I often think he isn't ———, but he seems to ——— what I say.

I ——— him talk, but I'm not sure I understood what he said.

Because I wasn't ———, I didn't ——— the instructions.

You ——— what I said; now do it.

Most of the time he just doesn't ———.

If you can ——— above all this noise, you're better than I am.

Why don't you just be quiet and ——— for a change?

You'll never believe what I ——— yesterday.

Most of the time he just doesn't ——— a thing I say.

If you want to ——— to what he has to say, come over
here where you can ——— better.

Do you think he ——— what was said?

He never ——— to me anyway.

6 I

My moods ——— often changed by the weather.	are
The boat must always ——— covered with a tarp.	be
My parents ——— still pressured by their friends.	are
We ——— constantly bothered by mosquitoes while we were there.	were
The sky ——— frequently spotted with clouds.	is (was)
I ——— tossed by the waves for hours.	was
You ——— still thought to be wise by your friends.	are
I ——— frequently warmed by the sun's rays.	am
The flowers ——— watered every day.	are
All of the books ——— read by the students.	were (are)
The last time he went riding he ——— thrown by a horse.	was
The papers should ——— picked up before long.	be
I ——— nearly driven to distraction by the noise he made.	was
The food ——— usually gone an hour after it's served.	is
One of the boys ——— hurt during the game.	was

7 A   **review of *be***
(all previous forms)

He knew he would have to do the work or he would ——— replaced.	be
Both he and his wife ——— coming.	are
I'll try to come, but I ——— not sure I can make it.	am

VERB FORMS

Steps in the verb forms category are restricted to the verbs *be* and *have*, the verb auxiliaries *be, have,* and *do,* and the modals on the assumption that students who have mastered these forms will have few, if any, problems selecting the correct form of other verbs when they are writing English sentences. However, in addition to these verbs, auxiliaries, and modals, there is one step in the verb forms section that has negative clozure and one step that has a tag question clozure. These are included because each calls for a knowledge of whether or not the auxiliary *do* should be included with the verb or verb group clozure of the sentence. The emphatic *do* has also been included in the steps.

STEPS

1. verb *be* present—am, are, is
2. verb *be* past—was, were
3. verb *be* present and past—am, are, is, was, were
4. auxiliary *be* with V-ing—is, was, am, are
5. verb *be* with auxiliaries and modals—be, being, been
6. *be* as passive auxiliary with past participle of verb—is, was, been, being, be
7. review of *be* (all previous forms)
8. verb *have*—have, has, had
9. auxiliary *have*—have, has, had
10. verb *have* with auxiliaries and modals—have, has, had
11. review of *have*—have, has, had
12. *be* and *have* as either verbs or auxiliaries—am, are, is, was, were, be, been, being, has, have, had
13. *be* and *have* in combinations as verbs and auxiliaries—has had, has been, had been, is having, are having, am having, was having, were having, had had
14. modals, present—can, shall, may, will, must
15. modals, past—could, should, might, would
16. modals, present and past—can, could, shall, should, may, might, will, would, must
17. review of all forms previously given
18. *do* as auxiliary—do, does, did

I.D. pictures will ——— taken tomorrow morning.	be
The theme ——— changed by the committee at the last meeting.	was
——— you raised by your parents?	Were
I ——— sunburned when I got home from the beach.	was
The bananas ——— stolen by someone in the neighborhood.	were
The rocks ——— shaded all day long.	are (were)

6 H

The grass ——— frequently trampled by the cows.	is (was)
The bananas ——— all eaten last night.	were
The candy ——— eaten before the movie started.	was
This year the games will always ——— played after dark.	be
The food ——— eaten before the prayer ——— said.	was; was
The dresses ——— torn when she got them.	were
Clouds ——— frequently full of rain.	are
Even now, I ——— still being teased by my friends.	am
The children ——— always frightened by thunder.	are
This textbook has ——— used.	been
The food ——— eaten quickly.	was
Betty and I ——— surprised at the results.	were
They have ——— gone for over a year.	been
The book ——— left on the table.	was

19. negatives—forms—don't, doesn't, didn't, hasn't, haven't, hadn't, isn't, aren't, wasn't, weren't, won't, wouldn't, can't, couldn't, shouldn't, with present or past forms when negative is given by never, neither, etc.
20. question tags
21. subjunctive forms
22. review of all forms given

1 A

verb *be* present—
am, are, is

I ——— a student at the present time.

They ——— in class every day.

She ——— not a nurse.

We ——— in the band together and really enjoy our association there.

It ——— on the shelf and should remain there.

You ——— sad, aren't you?

They ——— not good students, but they try hard.

He ——— a doctor, not a teacher.

The mountains ——— pretty in the fall when the leaves turn color.

She ——— a good child and gives me very little trouble.

One of the boys ——— ill, and won't be here today.

Half of the apples ——— bad and we should throw them away.

This water ——— good to drink and I ——— very thirsty.

Half of this apple ——— bad and I can't eat it.

They should ——— notified about the change.   be

They were ——— hounded by their creditors because of their   being
unpaid bills.

The screws ——— attached to the chair seats.   are (were)

The hook ——— attached to the line before the bait is put on.   is

He has ——— questioned about the event.   been

Half of the apple ——— eaten earlier.   was

I'd like to go, but it hasn't ——— suggested.   been

A graph ——— needed to complete the project.   is

Bread and butter ——— furnished free with the meal.   was (is)

Half of the enemy troops ——— routed by our forces.   were

They were ——— fed by the Red Cross.   being

The students hoped they would ——— promoted by the   be
committee.

Why haven't these broken boxes ——— fixed?   been

6 G

My foot ——— bruised in the fall.   was

The paints ——— already mixed when we bought them.   were

The puppy ——— teased by the children.   was (is)

My teeth ——— polished yesterday at the dentist's.   were

The eggs ——— boiled for three minutes.   were

The swimmers ——— frightened by the shark yesterday.   were

The shark ——— also frightened by the swimmers.   was

We ——— shocked by the pictures we saw.   were

It ——— written by her father last year.   was

1 B

Here, with the other papers ——— the contract to sign.

Fresh bread and butter ——— good when we're hungry.

Pie and ice cream ——— my favorite dessert.

About half of the report ——— wrong and will have to be rewritten.

The wear and tear ——— too great on this job; I think I'll quit.

A table or graph ——— needed to help explain the figures or people will misunderstand.

Half of them ——— here already.

John, as well as the other boys ——— on the job.

The news in this paper ——— good.

In this file ——— all the records of the students.

In that group ——— the students from the United States; the others are in here.

Not only appearance, but also behavior, ——— important.

Any of those ——— suitable.

Mathematics ——— still an easy subject for me.

See if one of the apples ——— still good.

1 C

The news from home ——— usually good.

The people ——— here and ready to go to work.

This water ——— good to drink.

I'm afraid he's ――― delayed by the storm.   been (being)

The series of events ――― scheduled for next month.   is

6 E

All of the folders ――― completed early.   were

Some food ――― now being prepared by the committee.   is

Each folder ――― completed by hand.   is

It has ――― sent by airmail.   been

Mr. Jones ――― promised the job.   was

They said the books were ――― completed then.   being

It is ――― sent by airmail.   being

Spaghetti and meatballs ――― prepared by the committee.   was

A table or graph ――― needed.   is

He has ――― commended for his actions.   been

The boys ――― scolded by their parents.   were

Each item ――― inspected carefully at the factory.   was

I haven't ――― asked yet.   been

A series of performances ――― scheduled for fall.   was

Neither Mary nor John ――― permitted to play last night.   was

6 F

The group ――― committed to that policy.   was (is)

He has ――― called to be the chairman.   been

Four of the boys ––– on their way.

Half of the apple ––– bad and can't be eaten.

Rice ––– a staple food in the Orient.

Half of the group ––– ready to go already.

This group of boys ––– ready if the other group ––– not.

Some of the goods ––– usually damaged in transit.

The folder of reports ––– in the file here by my desk.

Few men ––– as happy as he –––.

Enclosed ––– your copies of the lease for your new rental.

Economics ––– a hard subject for almost everyone.

1 D

I ––– a businessman and live here in the city.

You ––– a friend of mine; that ––– why I'm advising you.

People ––– often funny.

––– you frightened?

––– he dependable in the face of danger?

I ––– not myself tonight.

Nothing in life ––– ever free.

The best things ––– always earned.

They ––– all friends of mine.

I ––– taller than you –––, so should outreach you.

He ––– a good swimmer, so he should win the race.

John ––– our oldest son.

I ––– always happy to see you.

We ——— struck twice by falling branches and could have ——— severely injured.   were; been

The beauty queen and her court ——— selected by the judge.   were

One of the spelling words ——— missed by a contestant.   was

Will the car ——— fixed in time for the trip?   be

They ——— mixed up in their directions.   were

The boys ——— warned several times.   were

The flag ——— hoisted high up on the flagpole.   was

They found that the food had already ——— eaten.   been

The race ——— run in record time although one of the best runners ——— disqualified.   was; was

6 D

I am honored to have ——— asked to speak.   been

He may have ——— called out of town.   been

All of the items ——— on sale.   were

Some of the problems on that test ——— very hard.   were

Everyone in the class ——— invited to the party.   was

Either Mary or her parents ——— expected to attend.   were

Each of the items ——— marked down.   was

One of the copies ——— damaged in transit.   was

I'd go, but I haven't ——— asked.   been

He is ——— sent to a new school next week.   being

They ——— tormented by mosquitoes on their canoe trip.   were

John is ——— promoted tomorrow.   being

Both students ——— selected to speak at graduation.   were

1 E

He ——— a doctor and knows what to do.

I know it ——— true; I've proved it several times.

Here ——— his books; will you take them to him?

John and Mary ——— at church, but they'll be home soon.

Everyone ——— present, so let's begin.

Where ——— the Temple located? We'd like to see it.

The books ——— there on the table; take what you want.

The children ——— outside now.

William ———n't here, but we expect him soon.

Here ——— his book.

I ——— not sure about that; I'd better look it up.

He ——— usually a good boy.

——— anyone there yet?

No one ——— here.

Everyone ——— here; let's begin.

1 F

——— you finished, so we can leave?

It ——— a beautiful piece of sculpture; I think I'll buy it.

There he ———, grab him.

Who ——— you and what do you do for a living?

She ——— a lovely dancer when you see her on the stage.

6 B

I ——— touched by his kindness.	was
One of the best cups ——— broken at the party.	was
The child ——— placed in a foster home.	was
The baby ——— adopted.	was (is)
The food had ——— burned earlier.	been
All the students ——— notified before.	were
They should ——— notified in time and make arrangements to come.	be
Several of the boys ——— advised to leave the area.	were
All the food ——— eaten rapidly.	was
He is ——— called to attend all the meetings.	being
One of the boys ——— asked to leave.	was
The area ——— contaminated by the atomic bomb.	was
The people ——— removed from the area.	were
All the students had ——— notified before the meeting.	been
Several bombs had ——— exploded previously.	been

6 C

They ——— given some free tickets to the show.	were
One of the performers ——— given a standing ovation.	was
Paper ——— scattered all over the fairgrounds.	was
He has ——— elected president two times.	been

Where ——— all the birds going to at this season?

I ——— a friend of Paul's; he asked me to deliver this message.

There ——— many students absent today.

There ——— the door; why don't you leave?

He ——— still a friend of mine.

They ——— still good friends.

——— I the leader or is he?

She ——— a thoughtful roommate and I appreciate her.

Which of the boys ——— your brother?

Both of the girls ——— here.

1 G

I ——— an athlete who competes in all the games.

We ——— friends even though we often quarrel.

You ——— an intelligent person and should make the right decisions.

Susan ——— in front so she can't hear you.

He ——— busy at the moment.

These ——— nickels, but they ———n't worth much.

I ——— thoroughly confused and don't know what to do.

What ——— the matter with everybody today?

My parents ——— here and I must leave with them.

——— she the one for the job or should we hire someone else?

——— this your first time here?

Mary has always ——— late, but she could ——— on time if   been; be
she wanted to.

I've only ——— here for two months.   been

It's ——— raining all week.   been

6 A   *be* as passive auxiliary
                    with past participle of verb—
                    is, was, been, being, be

The people ——— drenched by the rain.   were

The papers ——— picked up an hour ago.   were

The party ——— ended by the police.   was

The button ——— sewn onto the shirt.   was

The children ——— being scolded by their teacher.   were

My thoughts ——— often distracted by the waves.   are

My friend ——— delayed by traffic.   was

My dog ——— hit last night.   was

The old books ——— usually pushed aside in favor of the new.   are

During the last game the ball ——— hit only three times.   was

The game should always ——— played fairly.   be

The water ——— stirred by the wind.   is (was)

I ——— often influenced by my friends.   am

At the last hunt, the foxes ——— chased by the dogs.   were

I know that the speaker ——— heard by everyone there.   was

Why ––– you so shy when you meet people?

He ––– almost as tall as I ––– and may be taller before long.

2 A   verb be past—
was, were

It ––– a beautiful day when we left.

Because one of the boys ––– such a good player, we won.

Although we ––– late the show wasn't over.

Both of the boxes ––– open when he brought them.

He ––– ill and unable to attend the opening night.

Most of this apple ––– bad when I cut into it.

They said they ––– happy about it.

She ––– a good teacher when I ––– there at school.

Most of the apples ––– already bad.

Her parents ––– excited at the game last week.

He ––– mad at me because I did it.

Peanut butter and jelly ––– his favorite food.

That girl ––– very shy when it ––– her turn on the program last night.

There have ——— several accidents on that road.	been
She thinks we should ——— perfect.	be
I'd go but I've ——— there before.	been
He has ——— a lot of trouble, although he can ——— good when he tries.	been; be
What will you ——— doing tonight?	be
The sea has ——— rough ever since we arrived.	been
John has ——— in business since he graduated.	been
Has the postman ——— here today?	been
Should all the participants ——— here for the rehearsal?	be

5 F

Has she ——— sitting here all afternoon?	been
Where could he ——— going?	be
He is ——— obstinate again.	being
My father said he would ——— here tomorrow.	be
He has ——— playing tennis for an hour.	been
He hasn't ——— around here for a long time.	been
The telephone has ——— out of order for the past few days.	been
He might ——— here tomorrow.	be
He may have ——— too late for the show.	been
He was ——— troublesome when he did that.	being
The boat has ——— missing for a long time.	been

2 B

All of the items ——— on sale.

Some of the problems ——— hard on that test.

Years ago when I ——— young, football and hockey ———
my favorite sports.

The bundle of papers ——— on top of the load of things
you sent.

Where ——— you when I needed you?

John and Mary ——— late for school this morning.

Nobody ——— at the show last night.

Either Mary or her parents ——— there last week.

Each of the boys ——— absent at least once during the
semester.

Either her parents or Mary ——— there last week.

Those ——— the papers I needed yesterday.

Each of the items you sent ——— perfect.

Both John and Mary ——— at the program Tuesday.

I ——— not there when he came.

2 C

When ——— they married?

He ——— not as fast as I was.

I ——— excited when I read your letter.

We saw no rings that ——— as beautiful as mine.

I ——— younger then.

5 D

Where have you ——— for the past hour?	been
He could ——— an A student if he tried.	be
They should ——— here soon.	be
They should have ——— here long ago.	been
He was ——— charitable when he suspended the fine.	being
Some of them have ——— here before.	been
He has always ——— a good student.	been
Why can't you ——— like your sister?	be
There hasn't ——— anyone around for a long time.	been
They should have ——— here long before now.	been
Will you ——— at home tomorrow?	be
There hasn't ——— any trouble around here for quite a while.	been
He has ——— listening to the concert for the past hour.	been
Haven't you ——— to the store yet?	been
I'm afraid he's ——— difficult again.	being

5 E

He must ——— crazy to do that.	be
The show has ——— there for the past two weeks.	been
John should ——— here soon.	be
He is ——— obstinate.	being
She could ——— an excellent student if she wanted to.	be

——— that the first time you came here?

John ——— everyone's favorite yesterday.

The union ——— on strike two months ago.

At the last meeting the administrators ——— furious.

He ——— a cute puppy, but our dog is ugly now.

——— green your favorite color until you changed to red?

The cookies ——— in the kitchen, but someone has eaten them.

Where ——— you when the power went off?

He ——— a good ball player until he hurt himself.

We enjoyed ourselves while we ——— in Japan.

2 D

——— your father in Hawaii in 1947?

The car ——— green, but I painted it blue.

How long ago ——— you in Japan?

——— you there long?

What ——— the reason you left early last night?

I ——— a good dancer when I was young.

Did you hear what the correct answer ———?

I could not hear because it ——— too noisy in the dorm.

The neighbors ——— mad at us for two months.

I ——— in the wrong, so I apologized.

——— they on time or did they arrive late?

It ——— threatening rain so I left early.

Can you ——— at the meeting tomorrow?	be
He said he might ——— late.	be
The president has ——— reelected.	been
I may ——— leaving in a few minutes.	be
How can he ——— so careless?	be
There have ——— too many errors made.	been
Has she ——— notified about the meeting?	been
There have ——— meetings already.	been

5 C

How many people have ——— notified?	been
Could John ——— here by nine o'clock?	be
We must ——— very careful.	be
Why is he ——— so difficult?	being
There shouldn't ——— any problems while I'm here.	be
How could they have ——— so careless?	been
How long has it ——— since you were here last?	been
He will ——— the new president.	be
There have ——— many changes here.	been
She has ——— in school since September.	been
Haven't they ——— here for two weeks?	been
What would ——— the cost of such a program?	be
Why hasn't Mr. Brown ——— notified?	been
He said he would probably ——— late.	be
He has ——— waiting for a long time.	been

The water ——— warmer than the sand yesterday.

My parents ——— surprised to see me last Christmas.

The papayas ——— ripe so I picked them.

2 E

He ——— here yesterday.

It ——— an old house before they remodeled it.

They ——— surprised to hear the news.

She ——— able to do the work until she got sick.

Mary ——— happy when she heard about it.

Mary and John ——— there, too, and helped everyone.

I ——— sick yesterday.

You ——— the best speaker at the assembly a week ago.

One of the teachers ——— absent for three days.

I ——— not able to attend the last conference.

When ——— you there last?

You ——— in school then.

I ——— ready to go last week.

One of the boxes ——— open when it came.

My mother and father ——— there first.

5 A   verb *be* with auxiliaries and modals— *be, being, been*

We have ——— waiting for a long time.	been
He could ——— an A student if he tried hard.	be
He has ——— a teacher there for several years.	been
He is ——— as good as he knows how to ———.	being; be
She has ——— very little trouble to me.	been
They might ——— late, so we'd better not wait.	be
They have ——— gone a long time.	been
It could have ——— a real tragedy.	been
The train has ——— delayed for an hour.	been
There has ——— so much rain lately that everything is soaked.	been
It seems like he's ——— away for months.	been
They could ——— delayed for hours if the road has ——— washed out.	be; been
They have ——— here for about an hour.	been

5 B

He has ——— here a long time.	been
It could ——— an exciting game.	be
He is ——— his usual self-centered self.	being
She may ——— there next week.	be
We should always ——— on time.	be
There have ——— several meetings held there.	been
I haven't ——— there for years.	been

2 F

I ——— with Sione yesterday.

——— you at the dance last night?

He ——— a good friend of mine until he robbed the bank.

I think the party ——— fun last night.

My parents ——— upset when I phoned.

I am not as tall as you ——— at my age.

The picture we saw last night ——— terrible.

Mary ——— a good girl at school this morning.

I ——— not able to be in class yesterday.

The students ——— discouraged after the exam.

The beach ——— beautiful every day last week.

——— they excited over the news they received?

——— she with you last night?

What ——— the matter with her last night?

She ——— pretty when she was young.

3 A   verb *be* present and past—
                      am, are, is, was, were

Spaghetti and meatballs ——— the main dish for the dinner we gave.

Fresh bread and butter ——— good to eat.

The president ――― resting for a few minutes but will be here presently.   is

The students ――― listening to the teacher so they could pass the test.   were

My brother ―――n't attending school at present.   is

It ――― raining hard at the moment.   is

Most of the students ――― sleeping when the earthquake occurred.   were

4 F

One of the students ――― taking a typing course this semester.   is

The president ――― giving a speech next week.   is

Mr. and Mrs. Jones ――― going to Samoa next month.   are

They thought they ――― going to fly, but ――― taking a boat instead.   were; are

All of the girls ――― leaving tonight.   are

I ――― hoping he would come early.   was

How many of the students ――― planning on leaving?   are

See if John ――― coming.   is

My mother ――― bringing all her things with her when she comes.   is

The people at the party ――― talking and laughing when I left.   were

John ―――n't planning on it last week.   was

Both of them ――― arriving at once.   are

I ――― hoping he'll be here soon.   am

――― you sure she's coming at noon?   Are

All of the folders ——— ready now.

The winning boy or girl ——— fortunate.

In that group ——— many of the leaders.

Each of the folders ——— complete by itself.

There ——— something that really smelled good.

Only half of the group ——— here early.

The news ——— good.

The dessert ——— pie and ice cream.

Only half of the people ——— present.

The song and dance number ——— good; I think you'll
like it.

Half of the apple ——— good, so I ate it.

About a third of the students ——— prepared for the exam
when it was given.

Either Bill or John ——— absent yesterday.

3 B

——— he your little brother?

Yesterday, they ——— in the country.

I ——— not ready when he arrived.

Who ——— at the door now?

——— you happy at present?

I ——— ready to go when you are.

Scott ——— asleep on the couch; don't disturb him.

It ——— possible to be happy here if one doesn't dwell on
the past.

I ——— just wishing for some excitement when you came. was

They ——— learning to turn handstands when I saw them. were

I think the students ——— having a good time. are

Both of the boys ——— sliding on the slide when I saw them. were

Most of the students ——— having trouble with English this semester. are

I ——— sitting here waiting for the instructor to come in. am

No one ——— helping him set up all the things, so I tried to help. was

Mr. and Mrs. Brown ——— leaving on the tenth of the month. are

The two girls ——— visiting their grandmother this month. are

Either John or Mary ——— helping with this evening's program. is

She thinks Mary's mother ——— coming tonight. is

4 E

Some of the students ——— studying yesterday. were

One of the boys ——— teasing another one. was

Some people in the crowd ——— angrily shouting when the program ended. were

Neither Mary nor her mother ——— working yesterday. was

Both teams ——— trying hard to win this game as they are tied for first place. are

While one of the boys ——— speaking, the others ——— busy reading. was; were

The governor ——— running for the senate this year. is

Mary and her mother ——— shopping when they saw Bill. were

——— Miss Brown working on the report at this moment? Is

That ——— a mean thing you said last night.

It ——— clear a minute ago.

Verb games ——— fun.

What ——— your decision now?

I ——— sick all last week.

——— there any others absent yesterday?

I ——— a student in college at the present time.

3 C

Just as the sun ——— about to go down, the rain stopped.

——— you all in the same class now?

Why ———n't the teacher prepared yesterday?

I guess the sick men ——— not ready for that news last night.

What ——— the problem as the book states it?

I ——— almost done with this section.

I ——— not the one you are looking for.

There ——— many things to be done here.

What ——— the results of last week's quizzes?

You ——— to wait in the other room until I call you.

The banquet ——— at eight o'clock tonight.

Many of the people ——— in despair when they heard the news.

The blind ——— often taught to read Braille.

Braille ——— the means by which many blind people read.

Nowadays, news ——— transmitted instantaneously all over the world.

4 C

I ——— now reading books I have always wanted to read.	am
As far as I know, she ——— planning on teaching.	is
I ——— still coming home this summer.	am
He ——— trying for a scholarship but got an F.	was
The little girls ——— waiting outside if you want to see them.	are
The adults ——— drinking and singing so loud that I could not hear anything.	were
We ——— having our friends over for dinner next Sunday.	are
They ——— planning a beach party, but it rained.	were
We ——— considering finishing school this semester, but decided not to.	were
I ——— eating far too much these days.	am
——— it really snowing now?	Is
I ——— dreaming such a wonderful dream that I hated to wake up.	was
——— she wearing her sweater when you saw her?	Was
Most of them ——— thinking of quitting yesterday.	were
It ——— raining all the time we were there.	was

4 D

The children ——— having such a good time that I hated to interrupt them.	were
Earlier, some of the students ——— trying to fill out the reports while others ——— taking their health exams.	were; were
I hope the children ——— getting all the exercise they need.	are

3 D

The water ——— not nearly as warm yesterday as it ———
today.

The dogs ——— dirty when we bathed them.

Who ——— those girls you introduced me to?

Which dress ——— the cheapest before?

Where ——— your parents last night?

——— she happy to see you when you came?

One of the boys ——— absent yesterday without excuse.

My neighbors ——— at a party now.

——— he still a close friend of yours?

We ——— the best dancers in the show last year.

The tourists ——— silly when they arrived.

I ——— often afraid of the dark; even now.

——— your goal in life the same?

Sand ——— very colorful.

3 E

My homework ——— difficult yesterday.

The answers ——— hard to find, but I managed.

My roommates ——— too noisy for me to work last night.

I can tell that my teacher ——— home sick.

——— you always this noisy or can you be quiet?

The new house ——— beautiful.

We ——— driving to town this week.   are

We ——— still thinking of joining your group.   are

He ——— planning on attending college, but changed his   was
mind.

Earlier we ——— hurrying to catch the bus.   were

She ——— working with Dr. Fox last year.   was

4 B

They ——— having difficulty thinking of a reply before you   were
helped them.

Earlier he ——— crying, but he ——— fine now.   was; is

They ——— driving to town every day until the car broke   were
down.

He ——— making pizza last night.   was

I ——— presently taking English classes.   am

We ——— thinking of attending the play but stayed home.   were

I can see that he ——— running faster than the others.   is

I ——— considering changing my name, but decided not to.   was

The children ——— playing outside now.   are

I ——— writing as fast as I possibly can.   am

It ——— getting colder, so I shut the door.   was

I ——— still thinking of quitting school.   am

I could see they ——— trying to be good, but it ——— easier   were; was
to be bad.

Tell me what your future suggestions ———.

Which way ——— the bus stop?

Where ——— the bus going when it passed you?

That ——— a rare diamond you are wearing.

My sister and I ——— there last summer.

Many of the people ——— afraid.

He ——— an excellent student now.

She ——— unhappy when she left.

All my books ——— lost in the fire.

3 F

It ——— a long time ago when that happened.

There ——— several people present at the last meeting.

There ——— a nice tree in our yard and we enjoy its shade.

It ——— cold outside and warm in here.

There ——— many things wrong there, as there are here.

It ——— too bad about the accident; we're all sorry it happened.

It ——— late so we'd better go to bed.

There ——— a question about the decision, but it ——— settled now.

There ——— several jobs open last week, but I ——— not sure how many there ——— now.

There ——— some truth in that fact.

It ——— unexplainable why she doesn't study.

There ——— lots of errors in your paper and you will have to do it over.

There ——— a lot of noise at the meeting yesterday.   was

There ——— always a lot of noise at the meetings.   is

Where ——— the students? The room is empty.   are

It ——— impossible to do that; I've tried.   is

There ——— something in the air that smells good.   is

How many of the students ——— here?   are

There ——— many people present at the show last night.   were

There ——— some apples on the table.   are

Where ——— the student?   is (was)

4 A   auxiliary *be* with V-ing—
is, was, am, are

How many ——— planning to go dance in tonight's show?   are

Which of you ——— preparing for the future?   is (are)

We ——— going to the show last night, but ——— going   were; are
tonight instead.

Right now I ——— planning a party for next month.   am

——— you still thinking of a title for the book?   Are

You ——— talking with my father last night, weren't you?   were

Who ——— planning to ride with me tonight?   is

——— I serving the food?   Am

The children ——— making too much noise late last night.   were

3 G

——— the lessons easy this semester?

I ——— not very tired right now.

You ——— very late to the meeting last night.

It ——— in the bottom drawer; at least that ——— where I put it.

We've just had lunch so we ——— not very hungry.

There ——— a very difficult problem in that lesson.

What ——— the assignment for today?

Where ——— the lunch put?

This ——— a delightful experience.

That ——— the first time he ever did that.

We ——— too late to get in the movie last night.

Those ——— lovely pictures you have on the wall.

Bill ——— over there when I saw him last.

——— you ever on time?

3 H

It ——— amazing how much she can do.

It ——— raining yesterday.

There ——— several girls coming tomorrow.

Where ——— the post office located? I need to mail a letter.

There ——— some food on the table when I left.

It ——— a fact that the sun rises in the east.

3 G

——— the lessons easy this semester?	Are
I ——— not very tired right now.	am
You ——— very late to the meeting last night.	were
It ——— in the bottom drawer; at least that ——— where I put it.	is; is (was)
We've just had lunch so we ——— not very hungry.	are
There ——— a very difficult problem in that lesson.	is (was)
What ——— the assignment for today?	is
Where ——— the lunch put?	was
This ——— a delightful experience.	is
That ——— the first time he ever did that.	was
We ——— too late to get in the movie last night.	were
Those ——— lovely pictures you have on the wall.	are
Bill ——— over there when I saw him last.	was
——— you ever on time?	Are

3 H

It ——— amazing how much she can do.	is
It ——— raining yesterday.	was
There ——— several girls coming tomorrow.	are
Where ——— the post office located? I need to mail a letter.	is
There ——— some food on the table when I left.	was
It ——— a fact that the sun rises in the east.	is

There ——— a lot of noise at the meeting yesterday.

There ——— always a lot of noise at the meetings.

Where ——— the students? The room is empty.

It ——— impossible to do that; I've tried.

There ——— something in the air that smells good.

How many of the students ——— here?

There ——— many people present at the show last night.

There ——— some apples on the table.

Where ——— the student?

4 A   auxiliary *be* with V-ing—
is, was, am, are

How many ——— planning to go dance in tonight's show?

Which of you ——— preparing for the future?

We ——— going to the show last night, but ——— going tonight instead.

Right now I ——— planning a party for next month.

——— you still thinking of a title for the book?

You ——— talking with my father last night, weren't you?

Who ——— planning to ride with me tonight?

——— I serving the food?

The children ——— making too much noise late last night.

Tell me what your future suggestions ———.	are
Which way ——— the bus stop?	is
Where ——— the bus going when it passed you?	was
That ——— a rare diamond you are wearing.	is
My sister and I ——— there last summer.	were
Many of the people ——— afraid.	were (are)
He ——— an excellent student now.	is
She ——— unhappy when she left.	was
All my books ——— lost in the fire.	were

3 F

It ——— a long time ago when that happened.	was
There ——— several people present at the last meeting.	were
There ——— a nice tree in our yard and we enjoy its shade.	is
It ——— cold outside and warm in here.	is
There ——— many things wrong there, as there are here.	are
It ——— too bad about the accident; we're all sorry it happened.	is
It ——— late so we'd better go to bed.	is
There ——— a question about the decision, but it ——— settled now.	was; is
There ——— several jobs open last week, but I ——— not sure how many there ——— now.	were; am; are
There ——— some truth in that fact.	is
It ——— unexplainable why she doesn't study.	is
There ——— lots of errors in your paper and you will have to do it over.	are

We ——— driving to town this week.

We ——— still thinking of joining your group.

He ——— planning on attending college, but changed his mind.

Earlier we ——— hurrying to catch the bus.

She ——— working with Dr. Fox last year.

4 B

They ——— having difficulty thinking of a reply before you helped them.

Earlier he ——— crying, but he ——— fine now.

They ——— driving to town every day until the car broke down.

He ——— making pizza last night.

I ——— presently taking English classes.

We ——— thinking of attending the play but stayed home.

I can see that he ——— running faster than the others.

I ——— considering changing my name, but decided not to.

The children ——— playing outside now.

I ——— writing as fast as I possibly can.

It ——— getting colder, so I shut the door.

I ——— still thinking of quitting school.

I could see they ——— trying to be good, but it ——— easier to be bad.

3 D

The water ――― not nearly as warm yesterday as it ――― today.	was; is
The dogs ――― dirty when we bathed them.	were
Who ――― those girls you introduced me to?	were
Which dress ――― the cheapest before?	was
Where ――― your parents last night?	were
――― she happy to see you when you came?	Was
One of the boys ――― absent yesterday without excuse.	was
My neighbors ――― at a party now.	are
――― he still a close friend of yours?	Is
We ――― the best dancers in the show last year.	were
The tourists ――― silly when they arrived.	were
I ――― often afraid of the dark; even now.	am
――― your goal in life the same?	Is
Sand ――― very colorful.	is

3 E

My homework ――― difficult yesterday.	was
The answers ――― hard to find, but I managed.	were
My roommates ――― too noisy for me to work last night.	were
I can tell that my teacher ――― home sick.	is
――― you always this noisy or can you be quiet?	Are
The new house ――― beautiful.	is (was)

4 C

I ——— now reading books I have always wanted to read.

As far as I know, she ——— planning on teaching.

I ——— still coming home this summer.

He ——— trying for a scholarship but got an F.

The little girls ——— waiting outside if you want to see them.

The adults ——— drinking and singing so loud that I could not hear anything.

We ——— having our friends over for dinner next Sunday.

They ——— planning a beach party, but it rained.

We ——— considering finishing school this semester, but decided not to.

I ——— eating far too much these days.

——— it really snowing now?

I ——— dreaming such a wonderful dream that I hated to wake up.

——— she wearing her sweater when you saw her?

Most of them ——— thinking of quitting yesterday.

It ——— raining all the time we were there.

4 D

The children ——— having such a good time that I hated to interrupt them.

Earlier, some of the students ——— trying to fill out the reports while others ——— taking their health exams.

I hope the children ——— getting all the exercise they need.

That ——— a mean thing you said last night.   was

It ——— clear a minute ago.   was

Verb games ——— fun.   are

What ——— your decision now?   is

I ——— sick all last week.   was

——— there any others absent yesterday?   Were

I ——— a student in college at the present time.   am

3 C

Just as the sun ——— about to go down, the rain stopped.   was

——— you all in the same class now?   Are

Why ———n't the teacher prepared yesterday?   was

I guess the sick men ——— not ready for that news last night. were

What ——— the problem as the book states it?   is

I ——— almost done with this section.   am

I ——— not the one you are looking for.   am

There ——— many things to be done here.   are

What ——— the results of last week's quizzes?   were

You ——— to wait in the other room until I call you.   are

The banquet ——— at eight o'clock tonight.   is

Many of the people ——— in despair when they heard the   were
news.

The blind ——— often taught to read Braille.   are

Braille ——— the means by which many blind people read.   is

Nowadays, news ——— transmitted instantaneously all over   is
the world.

I ——— just wishing for some excitement when you came.

They ——— learning to turn handstands when I saw them.

I think the students ——— having a good time.

Both of the boys ——— sliding on the slide when I saw them.

Most of the students ——— having trouble with English this semester.

I ——— sitting here waiting for the instructor to come in.

No one ——— helping him set up all the things, so I tried to help.

Mr. and Mrs. Brown ——— leaving on the tenth of the month.

The two girls ——— visiting their grandmother this month.

Either John or Mary ——— helping with this evening's program.

She thinks Mary's mother ——— coming tonight.

4 E

Some of the students ——— studying yesterday.

One of the boys ——— teasing another one.

Some people in the crowd ——— angrily shouting when the program ended.

Neither Mary nor her mother ——— working yesterday.

Both teams ——— trying hard to win this game as they are tied for first place.

While one of the boys ——— speaking, the others ——— busy reading.

The governor ——— running for the senate this year.

Mary and her mother ——— shopping when they saw Bill.

——— Miss Brown working on the report at this moment?

All of the folders ——— ready now.	are
The winning boy or girl ——— fortunate.	is
In that group ——— many of the leaders.	are (were)
Each of the folders ——— complete by itself.	is
There ——— something that really smelled good.	was
Only half of the group ——— here early.	was
The news ——— good.	was (is)
The dessert ——— pie and ice cream.	was (is)
Only half of the people ——— present.	are (were)
The song and dance number ——— good; I think you'll like it.	is
Half of the apple ——— good, so I ate it.	was
About a third of the students ——— prepared for the exam when it was given.	were
Either Bill or John ——— absent yesterday.	was

3 B

——— he your little brother?	Is
Yesterday, they ——— in the country.	were
I ——— not ready when he arrived.	was
Who ——— at the door now?	is
——— you happy at present?	Are
I ——— ready to go when you are.	am
Scott ——— asleep on the couch; don't disturb him.	is
It ——— possible to be happy here if one doesn't dwell on the past.	is

The president ——— resting for a few minutes but will be here presently.

The students ——— listening to the teacher so they could pass the test.

My brother ———n't attending school at present.

It ——— raining hard at the moment.

Most of the students ——— sleeping when the earthquake occurred.

4 F

One of the students ——— taking a typing course this semester.

The president ——— giving a speech next week.

Mr. and Mrs. Jones ——— going to Samoa next month.

They thought they ——— going to fly, but ——— taking a boat instead.

All of the girls ——— leaving tonight.

I ——— hoping he would come early.

How many of the students ——— planning on leaving?

See if John ——— coming.

My mother ——— bringing all her things with her when she comes.

The people at the party ——— talking and laughing when I left.

John ———n't planning on it last week.

Both of them ——— arriving at once.

I ——— hoping he'll be here soon.

——— you sure she's coming at noon?

2 F

I ——— with Sione yesterday.	was
——— you at the dance last night?	Were
He ——— a good friend of mine until he robbed the bank.	was
I think the party ——— fun last night.	was
My parents ——— upset when I phoned.	were
I am not as tall as you ——— at my age.	were
The picture we saw last night ——— terrible.	was
Mary ——— a good girl at school this morning.	was
I ——— not able to be in class yesterday.	was
The students ——— discouraged after the exam.	were
The beach ——— beautiful every day last week.	was
——— they excited over the news they received?	Were
——— she with you last night?	Was
What ——— the matter with her last night?	was
She ——— pretty when she was young.	was

3 A   verb *be* present and past—
am, are, is, was, were

Spaghetti and meatballs ——— the main dish for the dinner we gave.	was
Fresh bread and butter ——— good to eat.	is

5 A   verb *be* with auxiliaries and modals—
be, being, been

We have ――― waiting for a long time.

He could ――― an A student if he tried hard.

He has ――― a teacher there for several years.

He is ――― as good as he knows how to ―――.

She has ――― very little trouble to me.

They might ――― late, so we'd better not wait.

They have ――― gone a long time.

It could have ――― a real tragedy.

The train has ――― delayed for an hour.

There has ――― so much rain lately that everything is soaked.

It seems like he's ――― away for months.

They could ――― delayed for hours if the road has ―――
washed out.

They have ――― here for about an hour.

5 B

He has ――― here a long time.

It could ――― an exciting game.

He is ――― his usual self-centered self.

She may ――― there next week.

We should always ――― on time.

There have ――― several meetings held there.

I haven't ――― there for years.

The water ——— warmer than the sand yesterday.   was

My parents ——— surprised to see me last Christmas.   were

The papayas ——— ripe so I picked them.   were

2 E

He ——— here yesterday.   was

It ——— an old house before they remodeled it.   was

They ——— surprised to hear the news.   were

She ——— able to do the work until she got sick.   was

Mary ——— happy when she heard about it.   was

Mary and John ——— there, too, and helped everyone.   were

I ——— sick yesterday.   was

You ——— the best speaker at the assembly a week ago.   were

One of the teachers ——— absent for three days.   was

I ——— not able to attend the last conference.   was

When ——— you there last?   were

You ——— in school then.   were

I ——— ready to go last week.   was

One of the boxes ——— open when it came.   was

My mother and father ——— there first.   were

Can you ––– at the meeting tomorrow?

He said he might ––– late.

The president has ––– reelected.

I may ––– leaving in a few minutes.

How can he ––– so careless?

There have ––– too many errors made.

Has she ––– notified about the meeting?

There have ––– meetings already.

5 C

How many people have ––– notified?

Could John ––– here by nine o'clock?

We must ––– very careful.

Why is he ––– so difficult?

There shouldn't ––– any problems while I'm here.

How could they have ––– so careless?

How long has it ––– since you were here last?

He will ––– the new president.

There have ––– many changes here.

She has ––– in school since September.

Haven't they ––– here for two weeks?

What would ––– the cost of such a program?

Why hasn't Mr. Brown ––– notified?

He said he would probably ––– late.

He has ––– waiting for a long time.

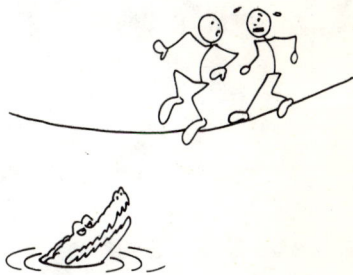

——— that the first time you came here?   Was

John ——— everyone's favorite yesterday.   was

The union ——— on strike two months ago.   was

At the last meeting the administrators ——— furious.   were

He ——— a cute puppy, but our dog is ugly now.   was

——— green your favorite color until you changed to red?   Was

The cookies ——— in the kitchen, but someone has eaten   were
them.

Where ——— you when the power went off?   were

He ——— a good ball player until he hurt himself.   was

We enjoyed ourselves while we ——— in Japan.   were

2 D

——— your father in Hawaii in 1947?   Was

The car ——— green, but I painted it blue.   was

How long ago ——— you in Japan?   were

——— you there long?   Were

What ——— the reason you left early last night?   was

I ——— a good dancer when I was young.   was

Did you hear what the correct answer ———?   was

I could not hear because it ——— too noisy in the dorm.   was

The neighbors ——— mad at us for two months.   were

I ——— in the wrong, so I apologized.   was

——— they on time or did they arrive late?   Were

It ——— threatening rain so I left early.   was

5 D

Where have you ——— for the past hour?

He could ——— an A student if he tried.

They should ——— here soon.

They should have ——— here long ago.

He was ——— charitable when he suspended the fine.

Some of them have ——— here before.

He has always ——— a good student.

Why can't you ——— like your sister?

There hasn't ——— anyone around for a long time.

They should have ——— here long before now.

Will you ——— at home tomorrow?

There hasn't ——— any trouble around here for quite a while.

He has ——— listening to the concert for the past hour.

Haven't you ——— to the store yet?

I'm afraid he's ——— difficult again.

5 E

He must ——— crazy to do that.

The show has ——— there for the past two weeks.

John should ——— here soon.

He is ——— obstinate.

She could ——— an excellent student if she wanted to.

2 B

All of the items ——— on sale.	were
Some of the problems ——— hard on that test.	were
Years ago when I ——— young, football and hockey ——— my favorite sports.	was; were
The bundle of papers ——— on top of the load of things you sent.	was
Where ——— you when I needed you?	were
John and Mary ——— late for school this morning.	were
Nobody ——— at the show last night.	was
Either Mary or her parents ——— there last week.	were
Each of the boys ——— absent at least once during the semester.	was
Either her parents or Mary ——— there last week.	was
Those ——— the papers I needed yesterday.	were
Each of the items you sent ——— perfect.	was
Both John and Mary ——— at the program Tuesday.	were
I ——— not there when he came.	was

2 C

When ——— they married?	were
He ——— not as fast as I was.	was
I ——— excited when I read your letter.	was
We saw no rings that ——— as beautiful as mine.	were
I ——— younger then.	was

There have ——— several accidents on that road.

She thinks we should ——— perfect.

I'd go but I've ——— there before.

He has ——— a lot of trouble, although he can ——— good when he tries.

What will you ——— doing tonight?

The sea has ——— rough ever since we arrived.

John has ——— in business since he graduated.

Has the postman ——— here today?

Should all the participants ——— here for the rehearsal?

5 F

Has she ——— sitting here all afternoon?

Where could he ——— going?

He is ——— obstinate again.

My father said he would ——— here tomorrow.

He has ——— playing tennis for an hour.

He hasn't ——— around here for a long time.

The telephone has ——— out of order for the past few days.

He might ——— here tomorrow.

He may have ——— too late for the show.

He was ——— troublesome when he did that.

The boat has ——— missing for a long time.

Why ——— you so shy when you meet people?   are

He ——— almost as tall as I ——— and may be taller before   is; am
long.

2 A   verb *be* past—
                          was, were

It ——— a beautiful day when we left.   was

Because one of the boys ——— such a good player, we won.   was

Although we ——— late the show wasn't over.   were

Both of the boxes ——— open when he brought them.   were

He ——— ill and unable to attend the opening night.   was

Most of this apple ——— bad when I cut into it.   was

They said they ——— happy about it.   were

She ——— a good teacher when I ——— there at school.   was; was

Most of the apples ——— already bad.   were

Her parents ——— excited at the game last week.   were

He ——— mad at me because I did it.   was

Peanut butter and jelly ——— his favorite food.   was

That girl ——— very shy when it ——— her turn on the   was; was
program last night.

Mary has always ——— late, but she could ——— on time if she wanted to.

I've only ——— here for two months.

It's ——— raining all week.

6 A   *be* as passive auxiliary
with past participle of verb—
is, was, been, being, be

The people ——— drenched by the rain.

The papers ——— picked up an hour ago.

The party ——— ended by the police.

The button ——— sewn onto the shirt.

The children ——— being scolded by their teacher.

My thoughts ——— often distracted by the waves.

My friend ——— delayed by traffic.

My dog ——— hit last night.

The old books ——— usually pushed aside in favor of the new.

During the last game the ball ——— hit only three times.

The game should always ——— played fairly.

The water ——— stirred by the wind.

I ——— often influenced by my friends.

At the last hunt, the foxes ——— chased by the dogs.

I know that the speaker ——— heard by everyone there.

Where ——— all the birds going to at this season?	are
I ——— a friend of Paul's; he asked me to deliver this message.	am
There ——— many students absent today.	are
There ——— the door; why don't you leave?	is
He ——— still a friend of mine.	is
They ——— still good friends.	are
——— I the leader or is he?	Am
She ——— a thoughtful roommate and I appreciate her.	is
Which of the boys ——— your brother?	is
Both of the girls ——— here.	are

1 G

I ——— an athlete who competes in all the games.	am
We ——— friends even though we often quarrel.	are
You ——— an intelligent person and should make the right decisions.	are
Susan ——— in front so she can't hear you.	is
He ——— busy at the moment.	is
These ——— nickels, but they ———n't worth much.	are; are
I ——— thoroughly confused and don't know what to do.	am
What ——— the matter with everybody today?	is
My parents ——— here and I must leave with them.	are
——— she the one for the job or should we hire someone else?	Is
——— this your first time here?	Is

6 B

I ——— touched by his kindness.

One of the best cups ——— broken at the party.

The child ——— placed in a foster home.

The baby ——— adopted.

The food had ——— burned earlier.

All the students ——— notified before.

They should ——— notified in time and make arrangements to come.

Several of the boys ——— advised to leave the area.

All the food ——— eaten rapidly.

He is ——— called to attend all the meetings.

One of the boys ——— asked to leave.

The area ——— contaminated by the atomic bomb.

The people ——— removed from the area.

All the students had ——— notified before the meeting.

Several bombs had ——— exploded previously.

6 C

They ——— given some free tickets to the show.

One of the performers ——— given a standing ovation.

Paper ——— scattered all over the fairgrounds.

He has ——— elected president two times.

1 E

He ——— a doctor and knows what to do.	is
I know it ——— true; I've proved it several times.	is
Here ——— his books; will you take them to him?	are
John and Mary ——— at church, but they'll be home soon.	are
Everyone ——— present, so let's begin.	is
Where ——— the Temple located? We'd like to see it.	is
The books ——— there on the table; take what you want.	are
The children ——— outside now.	are
William ———n't here, but we expect him soon.	is
Here ——— his book.	is
I ——— not sure about that; I'd better look it up.	am
He ——— usually a good boy.	is
——— anyone there yet?	Is
No one ——— here.	is
Everyone ——— here; let's begin.	is

1 F

——— you finished, so we can leave?	Are
It ——— a beautiful piece of sculpture; I think I'll buy it.	is
There he ———, grab him.	is
Who ——— you and what do you do for a living?	are
She ——— a lovely dancer when you see her on the stage.	is

We ——— struck twice by falling branches and could have
——— severely injured.

The beauty queen and her court ——— selected by the judge.

One of the spelling words ——— missed by a contestant.

Will the car ——— fixed in time for the trip?

They ——— mixed up in their directions.

The boys ——— warned several times.

The flag ——— hoisted high up on the flagpole.

They found that the food had already ——— eaten.

The race ——— run in record time although one of the best
runners ——— disqualified.

6 D

I am honored to have ——— asked to speak.

He may have ——— called out of town.

All of the items ——— on sale.

Some of the problems on that test ——— very hard.

Everyone in the class ——— invited to the party.

Either Mary or her parents ——— expected to attend.

Each of the items ——— marked down.

One of the copies ——— damaged in transit.

I'd go, but I haven't ——— asked.

He is ——— sent to a new school next week.

They ——— tormented by mosquitoes on their canoe trip.

John is ——— promoted tomorrow.

Both students ——— selected to speak at graduation.

Four of the boys ——— on their way.	are
Half of the apple ——— bad and can't be eaten.	is
Rice ——— a staple food in the Orient.	is
Half of the group ——— ready to go already.	is
This group of boys ——— ready if the other group ——— not.	is; is
Some of the goods ——— usually damaged in transit.	are
The folder of reports ——— in the file here by my desk.	is
Few men ——— as happy as he ———.	are; is
Enclosed ——— your copies of the lease for your new rental.	are
Economics ——— a hard subject for almost everyone.	is

1 D

I ——— a businessman and live here in the city.	am
You ——— a friend of mine; that ——— why I'm advising you.	are; is
People ——— often funny.	are
——— you frightened?	Are
——— he dependable in the face of danger?	Is
I ——— not myself tonight.	am
Nothing in life ——— ever free.	is
The best things ——— always earned.	are
They ——— all friends of mine.	are
I ——— taller than you ———, so should outreach you.	am; are
He ——— a good swimmer, so he should win the race.	is
John ——— our oldest son.	is
I ——— always happy to see you.	am

I'm afraid he's ——— delayed by the storm.

The series of events ——— scheduled for next month.

6 E

All of the folders ——— completed early.

Some food ——— now being prepared by the committee.

Each folder ——— completed by hand.

It has ——— sent by airmail.

Mr. Jones ——— promised the job.

They said the books were ——— completed then.

It is ——— sent by airmail.

Spaghetti and meatballs ——— prepared by the committee.

A table or graph ——— needed.

He has ——— commended for his actions.

The boys ——— scolded by their parents.

Each item ——— inspected carefully at the factory.

I haven't ——— asked yet.

A series of performances ——— scheduled for fall.

Neither Mary nor John ——— permitted to play last night.

6 F

The group ——— committed to that policy.

He has ——— called to be the chairman.

1 B

Here, with the other papers ——— the contract to sign.   is

Fresh bread and butter ——— good when we're hungry.   is

Pie and ice cream ——— my favorite dessert.   is

About half of the report ——— wrong and will have to be rewritten.   is

The wear and tear ——— too great on this job; I think I'll quit.   is

A table or graph ——— needed to help explain the figures or people will misunderstand.   is

Half of them ——— here already.   are

John, as well as the other boys ——— on the job.   is

The news in this paper ——— good.   is

In this file ——— all the records of the students.   are

In that group ——— the students from the United States; the others are in here.   are

Not only appearance, but also behavior, ——— important.   is

Any of those ——— suitable.   is

Mathematics ——— still an easy subject for me.   is

See if one of the apples ——— still good.   is

1 C

The news from home ——— usually good.   is

The people ——— here and ready to go to work.   are

This water ——— good to drink.   is

147

They should ——— notified about the change.

They were ——— hounded by their creditors because of their unpaid bills.

The screws ——— attached to the chair seats.

The hook ——— attached to the line before the bait is put on.

He has ——— questioned about the event.

Half of the apple ——— eaten earlier.

I'd like to go, but it hasn't ——— suggested.

A graph ——— needed to complete the project.

Bread and butter ——— furnished free with the meal.

Half of the enemy troops ——— routed by our forces.

They were ——— fed by the Red Cross.

The students hoped they would ——— promoted by the committee.

Why haven't these broken boxes ——— fixed?

6 G

My foot ——— bruised in the fall.

The paints ——— already mixed when we bought them.

The puppy ——— teased by the children.

My teeth ——— polished yesterday at the dentist's.

The eggs ——— boiled for three minutes.

The swimmers ——— frightened by the shark yesterday.

The shark ——— also frightened by the swimmers.

We ——— shocked by the pictures we saw.

It ——— written by her father last year.

19. negatives—forms—don't, doesn't, didn't, hasn't, haven't, hadn't, isn't, aren't, wasn't, weren't, won't, wouldn't, can't, couldn't, shouldn't, with present or past forms when negative is given by never, neither, etc.
20. question tags
21. subjunctive forms
22. review of all forms given

1 A   **verb *be* present—**
am, are, is

I ––– a student at the present time.	am
They ––– in class every day.	are
She ––– not a nurse.	is
We ––– in the band together and really enjoy our association there.	are
It ––– on the shelf and should remain there.	is
You ––– sad, aren't you?	are
They ––– not good students, but they try hard.	are
He ––– a doctor, not a teacher.	is
The mountains ––– pretty in the fall when the leaves turn color.	are
She ––– a good child and gives me very little trouble.	is
One of the boys ––– ill, and won't be here today.	is
Half of the apples ––– bad and we should throw them away.	are
This water ––– good to drink and I ––– very thirsty.	is; am
Half of this apple ––– bad and I can't eat it.	is

I.D. pictures will ——— taken tomorrow morning.

The theme ——— changed by the committee at the last meeting.

——— you raised by your parents?

I ——— sunburned when I got home from the beach.

The bananas ——— stolen by someone in the neighborhood.

The rocks ——— shaded all day long.

6 H

The grass ——— frequently trampled by the cows.

The bananas ——— all eaten last night.

The candy ——— eaten before the movie started.

This year the games will always ——— played after dark.

The food ——— eaten before the prayer ——— said.

The dresses ——— torn when she got them.

Clouds ——— frequently full of rain.

Even now, I ——— still being teased by my friends.

The children ——— always frightened by thunder.

This textbook has ——— used.

The food ——— eaten quickly.

Betty and I ——— surprised at the results.

They have ——— gone for over a year.

The book ——— left on the table.

VERB FORMS

Steps in the verb forms category are restricted to the verbs *be* and *have,* the verb auxiliaries *be, have,* and *do,* and the modals on the assumption that students who have mastered these forms will have few, if any, problems selecting the correct form of other verbs when they are writing English sentences. However, in addition to these verbs, auxiliaries, and modals, there is one step in the verb forms section that has negative clozure and one step that has a tag question clozure. These are included because each calls for a knowledge of whether or not the auxiliary *do* should be included with the verb or verb group clozure of the sentence. The emphatic *do* has also been included in the steps.

STEPS

1. verb *be* present—am, are, is
2. verb *be* past—was, were
3. verb *be* present and past—am, are, is, was, were
4. auxiliary *be* with V-ing—is, was, am, are
5. verb *be* with auxiliaries and modals—be, being, been
6. *be* as passive auxiliary with past participle of verb—is, was, been, being, be
7. review of *be* (all previous forms)
8. verb *have*—have, has, had
9. auxiliary *have*—have, has, had
10. verb *have* with auxiliaries and modals—have, has, had
11. review of *have*—have, has, had
12. *be* and *have* as either verbs or auxiliaries—am, are, is, was, were, be, been, being, has, have, had
13. *be* and *have* in combinations as verbs and auxiliaries—has had, has been, had been, is having, are having, am having, was having, were having, had had
14. modals, present—can, shall, may, will, must
15. modals, past—could, should, might, would
16. modals, present and past—can, could, shall, should, may, might, will, would, must
17. review of all forms previously given
18. *do* as auxiliary—do, does, did

6 I

My moods ——— often changed by the weather.

The boat must always ——— covered with a tarp.

My parents ——— still pressured by their friends.

We ——— constantly bothered by mosquitoes while we were there.

The sky ——— frequently spotted with clouds.

I ——— tossed by the waves for hours.

You ——— still thought to be wise by your friends.

I ——— frequently warmed by the sun's rays.

The flowers ——— watered every day.

All of the books ——— read by the students.

The last time he went riding he ——— thrown by a horse.

The papers should ——— picked up before long.

I ——— nearly driven to distraction by the noise he made.

The food ——— usually gone an hour after it's served.

One of the boys ——— hurt during the game.

7 A   **review of *be***
(all previous forms)

He knew he would have to do the work or he would ——— replaced.

Both he and his wife ——— coming.

I'll try to come, but I ——— not sure I can make it.

Most of the students have ——— the news.   heard

He was ——— to some music when I saw him last.   listening

He brought his radio so we could ——— to the broadcast,   listen;
but we couldn't ——— it very well as it was noisy on   hear
the beach.

Why don't we go and ——— the concert?   hear

If you had ——— carefully, you would have ——— what he   listened; heard
said.

What was it you ———?   heard

16 F

I often think he isn't ———, but he seems to ——— what I say.   listening; hear

I ——— him talk, but I'm not sure I understood what he said.   heard

Because I wasn't ———, I didn't ——— the instructions.   listening; hear

You ——— what I said; now do it.   heard

Most of the time he just doesn't ———.   listen

If you can ——— above all this noise, you're better than I am. hear

Why don't you just be quiet and ——— for a change?   listen

You'll never believe what I ——— yesterday.   heard

Most of the time he just doesn't ——— a thing I say.   hear

If you want to ——— to what he has to say, come over   listen;
here where you can ——— better.   hear

Do you think he ——— what was said?   heard

He never ——— to me anyway.   listens

He ——— unable to come, but he will send a substitute.

She wanted to help but she ———n't prepared.

I don't think I need to worry about it; however, it could ——— important.

He has ——— trying very hard to do what ——— right.

It could have ——— a disaster but everything turned out all right.

Everything would have ——— wonderful if you had ——— there.

They ———n't there.

He ——— overjoyed with the results.

Here ——— the results of the test.

Where have you ———?

7 B

He has ——— here since three o'clock.

Everyone ——— given a special assignment.

We were happy to ——— of assistance.

Where ——— you when he arrived?

It will soon ——— three hours since he arrived.

Their tasks ——— all finished on time.

Only one of the jobs ——— left to do.

They have ——— happy with their work.

He ——— being considered for an important position.

I ——— tired of hearing excuses every day.

She has ——— careful in her work.

16 D

Speak louder so I can ——— you.	hear
He only ——— to your side of the argument.	listened
He tried to ——— to everyone at once; consequently, he didn't ——— anything that made sense.	listen; hear
Why doesn't the chairman tell them to be quiet and ———?	listen
He tried to ——— what was being said, but it was impossible because of the noise.	hear
No one was ——— to anything anybody else was saying.	listening
Although he doesn't ——— a word I say, I think he understands.	hear
I ——— that too, but I refuse to believe it. I don't like ——— to gossip.	heard; listening
I really didn't ——— that announcement, but, you know, I really wasn't ——— very closely.	hear; listening
Where did you ——— that piece of news?	hear
I ——— very carefully, but I didn't ——— anything about it.	listened; hear

16 E

It seems to me that she only ——— what she wants to ———.	hears; hear
He should have ——— carefully to the instructions, and he might have ——— how to put it together.	listened; heard
Why don't we go and ——— to the concert?	listen
I don't think we can ——— in that part of the room, even if we ——— carefully.	hear; listen

It ――― often difficult to do what is right.

The meal ――― prepared quickly last night.

We ――― there for several hours.

We ――― warned not to go any further.

7 C

The table's surface ――― very smooth.

One of the boys ――― late last night.

The weather ――― better today than it ――― yesterday.

Where have you ―――?

Where can he ―――?

He ――― singing on the program tomorrow.

He will ――― here in an hour.

He ――― thankful for the food.

If we don't hurry, we'll ――― late for the party.

He hasn't ――― here very often.

It seems like we ――― always late.

One of the girls ――― injured by a fall.

Both of them ――― present at the meeting.

Where can that ――― found?

Be quiet! We're ——— to the news.

Although he ——— closely, he had trouble ——— the
speaker because of the surrounding noise.

That's the first time I've ever ——— that.

Why aren't you ——— to the teacher?

If the children want to ——— the story, they will have to
sit quietly on the floor.

If the children want to ——— to the story, they will have
to sit quietly on the floor.

listening

listened; hearing

heard

listening

hear

listen

16 C

You will have to ——— very carefully or you won't be
able to ——— the speaker.

She said she was ———, but she didn't ——— the
announcement.

He won't ——— to anyone but his mother.

I wonder why he didn't ——— to you.

He said he only came because he wanted to ——— the
main speaker.

I wish I hadn't ——— to him and ——— all the bad news.

He only ——— to one side of the proposition; he should
really ——— the other side too.

He said he was tired of ——— to all that chatter, so he
went for a walk so he didn't have to ——— it.

I think I'll relax and ——— to the radio for a while.

Oh, I ——— that a long time ago.

I don't repeat everything I ———.

listen;
hear

listening; hear

listen

listen

hear

listened; heard

listened;
hear

listening;
hear

listen

heard

hear

7 D

Everyone ——— happy about the party.

Either his friends or John ——— going to call on you.

Try and ——— on time for a change.

One of the girls ——— going to ——— the queen.

He would have ——— on time if they hadn't come.

Some of the books ——— missing yesterday.

He ——— selected by the committee.

Where have you ——— during the last hour?

Most of the students ——— surprised although they shouldn't have ———.

She ——— on her way to town when she ——— stopped by her friend.

He should ——— here by now.

Which one of the books ——— yours?

7 E

All of the students ——— present, but one of them ——— late.

We have ——— happy here.

Sometimes she ——— lonesome.

She has ——— late several times.

They should ——— here any minute now.

What ——— your opinion?

I must ——— there tomorrow.

16 A   listen, hear

You'll have to ——— carefully to ——— what he says.	listen; hear
I was sitting in the back and couldn't ——— what was said.	hear
I have to ——— to her every time she complains.	listen
Why didn't you ——— to what he said the first time?	listen
She thought she ——— him talking.	heard
I wouldn't ——— if I were you, as you won't ——— anything good.	listen; hear
I ——— her the first time.	heard
If you don't ———, you won't ——— the directions.	listen; hear
Why didn't you ——— to what he said the first time?	listen
Turn up the radio so I can ——— it.	hear
Turn on the TV; I want to ——— the news.	hear
Turn on the TV; I want to ——— to the news.	listen

16 B

Let's ——— to the concert tonight, but let's go early as you can't ——— in the back of the hall.	listen; hear
I didn't ——— her say that, but I really didn't ——— very closely.	hear; listen
Turn on the TV; let's ——— to the 5 o'clock news.	listen
Did you ——— anything interesting at the meeting?	hear
It seems to me he can ——— when he wants to.	hear
He told me about it after he ——— it.	heard

He ——— afraid he will ——— late for the meeting.

They ——— taken yesterday while we ——— gone.

He has ——— my best friend for years.

He is ——— sought by the police.

Where ——— he when I needed him?

7 F

All of the team members ——— hurt during the game.

He has ——— gone a long time.

He ——— frequently absent from class.

One of the apples ——— bad.

John, with his father, ——— present at the meeting.

Everyone but Mary ——— there.

The news ——— soon forgotten.

All of the class members except Mary ——— there.

There ——— too many errors on the paper, so John ———
told to rewrite it.

Where ——— John when it happened?

He should ——— here now.

There ——— a nice restaurant near here.

Have you ——— here before?

The boys ——— scolded for their actions.

You stay and ——— the game and I'll ——— if I can   watch; see
locate her.

All the travelers were ——— for their luggage as they   looking;
couldn't ——— it on the baggage cart.   see

She loves to ——— TV; she ——— at that screen all day.   watch; looks

She doesn't ——— very well today. Has she been sick?   look

I ——— her yesterday, and she ——— better than she did   saw; looks
then.

He's been ——— that show for an hour.   watching

15 F

Why don't you come over to my house and ——— TV   watch
with me?

I have something in my eye and can't ——— very well.   see

I wish he'd ——— at me once in a while; I really don't   look;
——— what he ——— in her.   see; sees

I want to ——— that new play everyone's talking about.   see

She didn't ——— at all startled when she saw him here.   look

Let's ——— and ——— what happens.   watch; see
                                                          (see; watch)

I wish you'd ——— over these plans and ——— what's   look; see
wrong with them.

I told her she'd better ——— sharp and ——— her actions   look; watch
or she'd be in trouble.

He wants to ——— the ball game so he'll ——— it on TV.   see; watch
                                                          (watch; see)

133

7 G

You should try and ――― on time tomorrow.

How long have you ――― here?

One of the boys ――― hurt yesterday.

He ――― going to try again tomorrow.

They ――― usually happy when they ――― here during the holidays last year.

He is ――― scolded by the instructor.

Some of these apples ――― bad.

Which of the girls over there ――― your friend?

When ――― he here last?

I saw several of the students who ――― waiting for the grades to ――― posted.

Which dessert ――― the best?

They had ――― in Europe before they ――― here last year.

8 A   verb *have—*
                                    have, has, had

He ――― several opportunities to perform while he was there.

She ――― lots of friends.

How many problems do you ――― to finish?

Her mother ――― several new books.

He ――― a cold, but he is better now.

15 D

I'll ——— the baby while you ——— to the other things.   watch; see

I ——— the accident happen and stayed until help arrived.   saw

Why doesn't he ——— where he is going? He could have ——— that car.   watch; seen

Everyone doesn't ——— things the same way.   see

I'd ——— my language if I were you.   watch

He's ——— this way; let's hope he——— us.   looking; sees

He asked to ——— over his homework to ——— if he had done it correctly.   look; see

Let's wait and ——— what happens when they ——— what he's done to the house.   watch (see); see

He ——— like he's mad at what he ———.   looks; sees

15 E

He ——— at her but didn't speak.   looked

He's been ——— her very closely all evening.   watching

It didn't ——— like he was going to make it, but he did.   look

He didn't ——— anything in it for him, so he left.   see

She's ——— all over for you.   looking

Be sure and buy everything we'll ——— to make pizza.   need

He should see a doctor as he ——— help.   needs

He just ——— some attention, so he's making a scene.   wants

12 E

The trees ——— watering today.   need

The whole country ——— rain.   needs

I don't ——— it to rain because we're having a picnic.   want

The children ——— some new clothes for the winter.   need (want)

He ——— you to come and see him.   wants

He's having a lot of trouble and ——— help.   needs

He ——— many things, but ——— only a few.   wants; needs

He said he ——— to be my friend.   wanted

Bring only the things you will ——— as we haven't much   need
room.

He is ——— by the police.   wanted

What does one ——— to do to join the club?   need

Where were you when I ——— your help?   needed

He ——— fried chicken.   wants (wanted)

I ——— some help or I won't get my work done.   need

10 D

We're ——— a late lunch.

She has ——— a hard time since she came here.

She is ——— some trouble with her assignments.

Mary might ——— your textbook.

I haven't ——— so much fun in years.

You haven't ——— enough practice.

His parents were ——— to send him money.

We should ——— time to stop by the library.

They have ——— a long time to think about it.

She's ——— some friends in tonight.

One of the contestants has ——— to withdraw.

When will you be ——— a party again?

I wish I could ——— a trip abroad while John wishes he
could ——— a new car.

We're ——— so much fun I don't want to leave.

10 E

He must ——— completed his work by now.

He says he hasn't ——— enough time to do it.

You should ——— known that.

We were ——— a good time until the neighbors complained.

You really should ——— more money than that.

She hasn't ——— that very long.

12 F

I ——— to go, but I ——— to save my money for next year's tuition.	want; need
How fast do you ——— to run to make the team?	need
I ——— to go to the party, but I wasn't invited.	wanted
Everyone ——— to help although we only ——— two people.	wants; need
She ——— to buy something, but she ——— to go to the bank first.	wants; needs
He ——— to leave on Monday to get there on time.	needs
She ——— fifteen dollars to buy the things she ———.	needs; wants (wants; needs)
Although I have everything I ———, I ——— a few luxuries too.	need; want
What do you ——— me to bring you?	want
They ——— ten thousand dollars to finish the project.	need

13 A   want, like

John ——— Mary; in fact, he ——— to marry her.	likes; wants
What would you ——— for dinner?	like
He ——— to do the right thing.	wants (likes)
He ——— football and soccer.	likes

Why hasn't he ——— the car fixed?

She may ——— a cold.

They haven't ——— a fight for a long time.

They have ——— time to finish the test.

John and Mary have ——— many interesting experiences.

He said I could ——— it if I wanted it.

10 C

Why hasn't he ——— notice of the meeting?

They could ——— a good time if they'd go.

They are ——— a meeting in the library.

I am ——— a few friends in for dinner.

He has ——— several chances to go abroad.

He could ——— some trouble with the car.

He is ——— trouble with his homework.

He might ——— it. Have you asked him about it?

He had ——— some trouble with the group before that.

John is ——— fun swimming in the surf.

She hasn't ——— any trouble for a long time.

Mary might ——— a cold, although she hasn't ——— one for
a long time.

I heard that they were ——— some trouble.

How much trouble have they ——— recently?

When do you ——— to eat?	want
He ——— to read poetry.	likes
I don't ——— bananas.	like (want)
What would you ——— to eat?	like
He says he doesn't ——— to go.	want (like)
What would they ——— me to bring?	like
Bring whatever you ——— to.	want
Most of the students ——— their teachers.	like
What do you ——— me to bring to the picnic?	want
What do you ——— to eat?	want

13 B

Do you ——— to serve dinner now?	want
Bring whatever you'd ——— to.	like
He ——— her when he first met her.	liked
She doesn't ——— my work.	like
He said he ——— to go to Europe last year.	wanted
The children ——— their new toys.	like
He ——— to see you before you leave.	wants
If you don't ——— to go, say so.	want
What do you ——— out of life?	want
Do you really ——— an education?	want
Do you really ——— to study?	like

They may ——— several children by now.

Mary has never ——— time to do it for me.

They are ——— a test in English today.

They haven't ——— many opportunities before.

She is ——— guests for dinner tonight.

He said he hadn't ——— enough notice.

They aren't ——— a Christmas party this year.

I think she has ——— enough time to finish the test.

She can ——— them if she wants them.

We're ——— another party next week.

He will ——— some of them made for me.

They have ——— a fight every night.

10 B

He has ——— a hard time in school.

They are ——— a party tonight and want to know if you have ——— an invitation.

We were ——— trouble with the generator, but it has been fixed.

He has ——— several cars in the past two years.

He can ——— some of them if he wants them.

We have always ——— a car.

I haven't ——— enough to do this past week.

They should ——— a copy of it.

I ––– to watch movies.	like
Would you ––– a ride?	like
He ––– to begin again.	wants
I have ––– one of them for years.	wanted

13 C

She called and said she ––– to see you tomorrow.	wanted
I would ––– to make an appointment for tomorrow.	like
Does your boss ––– you to go?	want
A baby ––– lots of attention.	wants
I'm not really sure what I'd ––– to do.	like
I ––– to go to the beach, but I'll have to complete this assignment first.	want
She's studying hard because she ––– to pass the test.	wants
What does he ––– me to do?	want
Bring whatever you ––– to bring.	want
He said he'd ––– to bring ice cream.	like
She said she ––– it well enough to buy it.	liked
What she ––– to do and what she has to do are two different things.	wants (likes)
She's studying hard because she'd ––– to pass the test.	like
I ––– to go, but I didn't have time.	wanted
She would have ––– to have gone, but she couldn't find the time.	liked

9 F

Bring all the things you ——— finished with you.

Ask him if he ——— completed the report.

He ——— worked on it in Tonga and ——— also worked on it since he came here.

The school board ——— given us permission to have a field trip.

He ——— made several canoes.

My father ——— often brought me to school.

Most of the things ——— been sold already.

Her friends ——— assisted her a great deal.

My friend ——— changed his mind about going with us.

Many of the things ——— been sold before we arrived.

John ——— changed his mind a dozen times.

He ——— studied English before he took my class.

He ——— hoped they would accept him, but they didn't.

All our things ——— been in storage for a long time.

10 A   verb *have* with auxiliaries
and modals—*have, has, had*

She hasn't ——— that very long.

She was ——— a good time when we saw her last.

John has ——— an accident.

13 D

I'd ——— to go; however, I can't	like
I've always ——— to read that book.	wanted
There are a lot of students who ——— to see you.	want
Most of the students ——— sports.	like
Would you ——— to take charge?	like
What would you ——— to do tomorrow?	like
He ——— to work.	likes (wants)
Most people ——— to succeed in life.	want
He ——— to borrow the car tomorrow.	wants
He ——— to see you about a loan.	wants
Where would you ——— me to put this?	like
Why don't you ——— her?	like
He ——— us to be there on time tomorrow; in fact, he'd ——— us to be there by three o'clock.	wants; like
How many of you ——— this plan?	like

13 E

He thought he'd ——— to see the film, but he ——— to read the book first.	like; wanted
How do you ——— my new dress?	like
I've always ——— one like it.	wanted
I ——— to travel and ——— to visit Japan some day.	like; want
He ——— to read the book because he ——— the film.	wants (wanted); liked

No one ——— turned in his paper yet.

One of the boys ——— gone to every game the team ———
played this year.

——— you driven a car before you came to America?

If you ———n't turned in your paper you'd better hurry and
get it in.

9 E

If your father ———n't been there he should go.

——— you been studying English long?

The postman ——— been here and left.

Where ——— you put your papers?

He ———n't read the assignment yet.

He ——— already driven my car before I gave him
permission to.

How many times ——— you attended class?

I ———n't ever traveled there.

She ———n't filled out the form yet.

He ——— taken the exam before the others did.

John ——— just received a package from home.

——— it started to rain before you arrived?

My grandmother ——— lived here all her life.

We ——— known that man for years.

My brother ——— already written his report.

Do you ——— playing football?   like

Which game do you ——— to play tonight?   want

He thought he ——— to play on the team, but he's   wanted
changed his mind.

Most students ——— sports.   like

He gets along well with everyone as he ——— people.   likes

I ——— to go to the beach, but it looks like I won't get   want;
what I ——— as long as it's raining.   want

13 F

She ——— pancakes and eats them for breakfast every day.   likes

He ——— to go home.   wants

What do you ——— to do tomorrow?   want

When would you ——— to go?   like

I think he ——— to see you.   wants

He said he ——— to see a movie.   wanted

Do you really ——— to eat raw fish?   want (like)

I don't even ——— to taste it.   want

He ——— to listen to classical music.   likes

Where do you ——— to sit at the concert?   want

Who ——— to go with me?   wants

He'd ——— to go swimming.   like

He ——— fifty dollars for his work.   wanted (wants)

Why do you ——— to go?   want

Either John or Mary ——— already completed the work
before I arrived.

He ——— been a teacher for years.

One of the boys ——— fallen overboard.

They ——— faced many problems but ——— solved them all.

Both John and Mary ——— completed their work.

Why ——— you done it this way?

We ——— always tried to satisfy our customers.

Most of the meal ——— been eaten before we arrived.

Several of them ——— already finished before the rest
started.

Bring me all the things Mary ——— done so far.

Most of the students ——— taken English in their own
countries.

9 D

——— you ever driven a car before?

——— she ever met him before the party?

It ——— begun to rain before I left the house.

What did he say after he ——— read the letter?

He ——— waited for a long time to come here.

Mary told me she ——— received a letter from her aunt.

He ——— traveled all through the Far East.

The whole class ——— read the text beforehand.

I ———n't met your sister yet.

What ——— you eaten today?

14 A   like, want, need

I would ——— to see you dance at the Polynesian Cultural Center.   like

His mother ——— her son to get a college education.   wants

The house ——— to be painted.   needs

He ——— to go to the concert.   wants

Would you ——— some envelopes? I have more than I ———.   like; need

When she grows up she ——— to be just like her mother.   wants

I would ——— a roast beef sandwich, please.   like

We ——— more money to survive.   need

I ——— more time to get this finished.   need

He ——— chicken for dinner tomorrow.   wants

We ——— to store food in case of famine.   need

We ——— to hurry because we ——— to go to the beach.   need; want

You ——— more help than I can give you.   need

14 B

He's ill and ——— to see the doctor.   needs

Did he ——— his present?   like

Why doesn't he ——— to help us?   want

He ——— to study even if he doesn't ——— to.   needs; want

We ——— to leave by ten if we expect to get there on time. need

Where do you ——— to go on your vacation?   want

9 B

She ——— spoken to me twice.

We ———n't seen her around for a long time.

I ——— been here several times.

They ——— traveled extensively.

Where ——— everyone gone?

Some students ——— already done all the assignments, so will have lots of free time.

One of the students ——— finished the first part of the assignment before the class started.

——— you heard the good news?

Someone ——— helped them before they came here.

Half of the class members ——— finished that assignment.

Everyone ——— finished, so all of you may go home.

What ——— you eaten for breakfast before you got sick?

Why ———n't you written your mother?

Why ———n't you written to your sister before the holidays?

Half of the class ——— finished the first part of the assignment.

9 C

He ——— spoken to the girl several times.

The two boys ——— been here for a long time.

He could have come if he ——— wanted to.

John ——— to sing when Mary plays the piano.   likes

They ——— ten thousand dollars before they can start to   need
build their new house.

When do you ——— to go away?   want (need)

The plants ——— water; they are wilting.   need

What would you ——— to bring for the picnic?   like

I'd ——— to leave now as I ——— to get home before dark.   like; want

Who do you ——— to invite?   want

14 C

He said he'd ——— to leave early.   like

Why does he ——— to leave early? He really doesn't ——— to.   want; need

Bring everything you'll ——— on the trip.   need

He ——— to visit his friends when he has free time.   likes

Bring what you ——— because it's pot luck.   want

How long do you ——— to stay?   want (need)

If possible, he would ——— to see you tomorrow.   like

What do you ——— for your journey?   need (want)

You will ——— some eggs to make custard.   need

Everyone ——— to be happy.   wants

You'll ——— a ticket to get in.   need

I think he would ——— to come too.   like

Although he ——— to come he couldn't.   wanted

He doesn't ——— to talk about it.   want

All of the students ——— to take English until they meet the requirements.

Either Mary or John ——— my English book last.

9 A   **auxiliary** *have—*
                          have, has, had

He ———n't spoken to me for a long time.

Why ——— you brought them to me?

He ——— been accustomed to luxuries before he came here.

Mary ——— never taken time to do it before we came.

Jane ——— been ill for the past week.

I ———n't attended class all week.

One of the boys ——— broken his leg.

John and Bill ——— finished the work before I came in.

Some of the boys ——— been hurt.

Either John or his father ——— come to see me every day during the past week.

Most of them ——— brought their things with them.

When we got there we found that one of the students ——— left his ticket home.

Mary, John, and George ——— all read the book before the class.

The students ——— come to wish you well in your new undertaking.

How many of you ——— read this book before?

14 D

How many times do I ——— to tell you?	need
Every living thing ——— water.	needs
He really ——— to see a doctor even though he doesn't ——— to.	needs; want
I would ——— to go with you.	like
He said he ——— to thank you for your gift.	wanted
Everyone ——— a friend.	needs
Most people would ——— more money than they have.	like
Bring her if you ——— to.	want
He ——— a job but doesn't ——— that one.	needs; want
Why don't you ——— her?	like
Do whatever you ——— to about it.	want
He'd ——— a better job.	like
Do whatever you'd ——— about it.	like

14 E

The dog ——— a bath; he smells!	needs
He ——— to play football and ——— to be on the team.	likes; wants
What would you ——— to do tomorrow? Most of us ——— to go to the beach.	like; want
He ——— some help or he won't get his work done.	needs

What ——— the most value in your life?

Each of us ——— his own opinion.

We ——— a wonderful time yesterday.

I ——— a complete set now.

Where ——— all the time gone?

It ——— three parts and needs another one.

The class ——— a plan.

Half of the apple ——— brown spots on it now.

I ——— a bad dream.

Half of the apples ——— spots on them now.

8 F

The group ———n't any time to wait for her.

John ——— a textbook, but he lost it.

Most of us ——— plans for the future, but we ———n't done anything about them.

The members of the group ——— their tickets already.

Everyone ——— a great time at the party last night.

——— the mailman come yet? I ——— a letter that must be mailed.

Mary ——— the measles so will miss two weeks of school.

Every semester many of the students ——— problems with English.

Some of the students ——— problems before they came.

When do you ——— time to see me?

She always ——— enough time to do the things she wants to do.

What do I ––– to do to join the club? I ––– to join.	need; want
What would you ––– for dinner tonight?	like
John ––– a hot dog while Mary ––– a hamburger.	wants; wants
What do we really ––– to take with us? I don't ––– to take anything we don't ––– to take.	need; want; need
What do you ––– to do tomorrow?	want (need)

14 F

He's always happy because he ––– everyone.	likes
How much money do you think he ––– to just get by?	needs
He is ––– by the police.	wanted
I'd ––– to do something that I really ––– to do for a change instead of something I really ––– to do.	like; want; need
Where were you when I ––– you to help me?	needed (wanted)
I'd ––– to go to the dance, and Mary ––– to go too.	like; wants
Bring anything you'd –––.	like
I ––– movies, don't you?	like
I don't ––– to ride, I ––– to ride.	need; want
I ––– to go too, but I just couldn't make it.	wanted
I ––– to study, or I'll fail the test.	need

8 D

——— he any experience in that field?

She ——— several of them at home now.

What do you ——— there?

She ——— several children before she went to school.

My car ——— a flat tire on the trip.

He should ——— some ideas.

We ———n't time to go now.

This door ——— a broken lock.

Come down when you ——— time.

One of the boys ——— a broken leg and couldn't go.

Everyone ——— his own problems.

At times, everybody ——— ideas.

Someone ——— the book before I did.

All of the boys ——— some money, so we won't have any problems.

Anyone ——— a chance to win, but only one boy won.

8 E

All of the boys ——— books.

His comments ——— a big effect on the decision.

One of the boys ——— a car we can use.

Some people ——— many problems.

Which of the boys ——— the accident?

15 A   look, watch, see

He never ——— television.	watches
Why do you want to ——— that program?	watch (see)
I can't ——— from here.	see
When do you think you will ——— him again?	see
He always ——— at the audience when he performs.	looks
He ——— the performance last night.	watched (saw)
I haven't ——— my brother for years.	seen
——— at those boys over there playing basketball.	Look
He tried to ——— three different games at the same time.	watch
What do you ——— in him anyway?	see
I'll ——— for it tomorrow.	look
——— those boys over there playing basketball?	See
He ——— TV every night; I don't know what he ——— in it.	watches; sees
He never ——— at her or spoke to her all evening.	looked

15 B

He sat and ——— at her picture for hours.	looked
He ——— over this way, but I don't think he ——— me.	looked; saw
She always ——— television.	watches
The average child in America ——— TV at least four hours a day.	watches
He didn't ——— everything he wanted to at the fair.	see
Let's ——— the next race.	watch

I ——— several new books at home.

They ———n't enough time now to finish their work.

Some of the students always ——— lots of problems.

8 C

Half of the picture ——— mud on it; we'd better clean it up.

If I ——— the choice, I'd go in a minute.

If he ——— a chance, he'll go.

How many ——— books and can start now?

One of the students ——— a cold and can't come.

What ——— that to do with it?

Half of the pictures ——— mud on them and need cleaning.

It ——— a pleasant smell; you'll probably like it.

Some of the students ——— colds and can't come.

One of the students ——— a cold and couldn't come.

He ——— better study or he'll fail the course.

Neither Mary nor her mother ——— time to do it before morning.

I didn't like it because it ——— an unpleasant odor.

Which of these ——— the best tone?

Both of them ——— a good tone.

Several of the students ――― their work with them.

One of the students ――― a cold last week.

Half of this apple ――― spots on it.

We ――― to go and see the doctor this afternoon.

Half of these apples ――― spots on them.

Half of the work ――― errors in it.

This semester some of the students on campus ――― cars.

One of them ―――n't a car now.

If you ――― time, come and see me.

We ――― to finish our work before we left.

8 B

This vase ――― a blemish and needs to be fixed.

It ――― a blemish so they sold it at half price.

He ―――n't any left when we arrived.

We ――― lots of time to finish our work before the period ended.

They ――― their books now and can start the lesson.

It ――― a blemish so they should sell it at half price.

Half of the rice ――― weevils in it.

I ――― headache and think I'll go and lie down.

Bring me some apples if you ――― any.

Half of these apples ――― worms in them.

He ――― five As and one B.

She ――― many problems with her house before she moved.

Let's wait a while and ——— if anything happens.   see

He's ——— at the report now.   looking

She ——— like her mother.   looks

He doesn't want to ——— that program, but wants to   watch;
——— another one.   watch (see)

Before crossing the street one should ——— out for cars   watch;
by first ——— one way and then the other.   looking.

From where we stood, we couldn't ——— the performance.   see

15 C

How many of the movies in the series have you ———?   seen

Do you like to ——— the people when they perform?   watch

He likes to ——— at picture books.   look

Bring the baby over, I'll ——— her for you.   watch

How many of them can you ——— from here?   see

I'd like to ——— the performance; let's stay and ——— it.   see; watch
          (watch; see)

Which kind of TV shows do you usually ———?   watch

After you've ——— the program, I'd like your opinion of it.   seen (watched)

We ——— the game for about an hour and then left.   watched

After he had ——— over the field he decided to stay and   looked;
——— the game.   watch

Did you ——— the game last week?   see (watch)

I spent all day long yesterday ——— for it.   looking

He always ——— the games on Monday nights.   watches